To MY SOCCER HEROES —

KATE, ELIZABETH AND JIM —

I P C TEAMS, 1977

FROM AN INTERESTED
SPECTATOR — DAD

CHRISTMAS. 1977

starting soccer

by Edward F. Dolan, Jr.

photographs by Jameson C. Goldner

Harper & Row, Publishers New York Hagerstown San Francisco London

starting
soccer
A Handbook for Boys & Girls

STARTING SOCCER: A Handbook for Boys and Girls
Text copyright © 1976 by Edward F. Dolan, Jr.
Illustrations copyright © 1976 by Jameson C. Goldner

FIRST EDITION

Library of Congress Cataloging in Publication Data
Dolan, Edward F., Jr.   1924–
      Starting soccer.

      SUMMARY: A guidebook to basic soccer skills and
team strategies, the different playing positions, and
practice mini-games and warm-up exercises.
      1.   Soccer—Juvenile literature.   [1.   Soccer]
I.   Goldner, Jameson C.   II.   Title.
GV943.25.D64   796.33'42   76–3838
ISBN 0–06–021682–4
ISBN 0–06–021683–2 lib. bdg.

This book is for Rose

acknowledgements

Many people were very helpful in the preparation of this book. My special thanks must go to Nancy Crampton, Richard B. Lyttle, and Barry Sheppard, all fine soccer enthusiasts. They have been most kind, and most generous with their time.

And a very particular thank-you to all the young people of San Francisco, San Anselmo, Corte Madera, and Marinwood, California, who played soccer for many hours so that their pictures could be taken for the book:

Sharon Abbett, Karen Baumsteiger, Cheryl Benson, Gary Benson, Brian Best, Ronnie Campbell, Jeff Carter, Alan Cook, Ann Crampton, Scott Crowell, Vincent DePasquale, Farrell Eckert, Mike Firenzi, Craig Fitzpatrick, Michael Ginter, Ken Gmeiner, Ellen Greer, Michael Hallett, F. Joseph Hass, Toni Heckert, Christine Heilmann, Mai Wei Kadner, Ian Kadner, Catherine Lennon, Susanne Lennon, Bradley Loel, David Metzger, Bernie Murphy, Bob Nicely, Paul O'Brien, Jeffrey Safford, Caroline Shaffer, Michael Shaffer, Robert Sheppard, Shane Stiver, Laura Taricco, Carlos Wells, and Jack Weingart.

contents

1
welcome to soccer

The white-shirted attackers come rushing deep into enemy territory, the ball whizzing along the ground as they kick it from one to another. The defenders, their red jerseys gleaming in the afternoon sun, steel themselves in front of the goal, ready to meet the onslaught, eager to take the ball away.

Suddenly the ball flies low to an attacker over near the side of the field. From there, it zooms to a teammate who has slipped in behind the defenders. With the agility of an acrobat, and without ever putting a hand on it, the teammate snares the ball and kicks it hard at a corner of the goal.

The goalkeeper lunges desperately to stop the ball.

But too late.

It flashes into the goal. . . .

Welcome to soccer.

When you put on shorts and jersey to join in action such as this, you're part of a game that has won fame on many counts.

First, soccer is a game that's recognized as the most popular team sport in the world. It is played in some 150 countries on all five continents. Its World Cup play, which has been called a "world-wide Super Bowl and World Series rolled into one," draws a TV and radio audience of nearly 900 million fans of all nationalities. For all of this century, soccer has been a part of the Olympic Games.

Second, soccer is one of the fastest and most strenuous games ever played on foot. There are two teams of eleven players each. They meet on a field that's somewhat larger than a football field. But here any similarity to football ends. Football's action is stop-and-start. Soccer's is continuous, and all players are in action eighty percent of the time.

The soccer ball scoots up and down the field almost non-stop. It goes from one team to the other constantly. One minute your team may be deep in enemy territory, attacking and trying to score a point. A moment later, you may be back upfield in front of your own goal, struggling to prevent a score.

Unlike football, soccer has no separate offensive and defensive units. When the ball changes possession, you keep right on playing. As in basketball, each player gets the chance to do *everything* —to play both offense (attack) and defense.

And soccer is basically a simple game. The rules are few and easily learned. The whole idea is to score points by driving the ball into the opposing team's goal. You earn one point for each goal made.

Finally, simple though it is, soccer is one of the world's most challenging games. For you *never* touch the ball with your hands or arms. You can't catch it as it flies through the air. You can't throw it. You can't pick it up and run with it. Instead, you move it along the field and try for points with many other parts of your body.

Your feet do most of the work. But not all of it. You also use your legs, knees, and thighs. Your stomach. Your chest. And even your head.

All this makes soccer different from any other game. Parts of your body that really never get a chance to "handle" the ball in other sports are put to work. Soccer is such a fascinating game to play and watch, no wonder it's a world-wide favorite.

It is also one of the oldest games in history. It began as *tsu tsu* (meaning "to kick a leather ball with the feet") in China about 2500 years ago, came to England with the Romans soon after the birth of Christ, and then spread to the rest of the world. It is called soccer today because its first official name in England was "Asso-

Illustration 1   In many countries, girls don't yet play soccer, but in America it's enjoyed by girls and boys alike. They play on separate teams in some leagues. In others, the teams are mixed.

ciation Football," soon shortened to "A-Soc." From there, it was a short step to the present "soccer."

Though a world-wide favorite, soccer is a new game to most Americans. As recently as ten years ago, it was practically unknown here. Our games have always been football and baseball. (Football, incidentally, comes from Rugby, a game that is an off-shoot of soccer.) But now Americans have "discovered" soccer and are flocking to it in the millions, as players and spectators.

Young people are especially fond of soccer. Not only is it full of good action, but it has a place for all who want to play. Your size doesn't matter. Are you too short for basketball? Too light for football? A shade too plump for track? Then soccer is for you. It can be played by anyone. There are positions on the team for players of all shapes and sizes.

To see just how unimportant size is, take a look at Pelé, the Brazilian star said to be the greatest player ever in the game. He's a man of medium height, under six feet tall.

Young people have also learned that they can play without great fear of being hurt. Though strenuous and challenging, soccer is a very safe game, for it is not a rough, body-contact sport like football. If you play wisely and alertly, injuries are few and far between, and most often minor.

American girls have found soccer a game in which they can compete on an equal basis with boys. Girls' swiftness and agility make them fine players, and they have swelled the ranks of soccer players by several million. In some areas, they play in all-girl leagues. In many others, girls and boys play together on the same team.

Finally, many young Americans have taken up soccer because its equipment is so inexpensive. You don't need helmets, shoulder pads, bats, or mitts. Soccer requires only a ball and a field or a vacant lot. Just shorts, a T-shirt, socks, and a pair of shoes that won't slip on the grass. If you wish, you can buy regular soccer shoes (they start at about $12); otherwise, your favorite sneakers will do fine.

Soccer is so popular, you'll have little trouble finding a team to join if you haven't found one already. They're sprouting up everywhere. Elementary schools, junior and senior high schools, and colleges everywhere are taking up the sport.

If it's not yet come to your school, then you'll surely find a number of leagues in your community or neighborhood. Most have teams for different age groups. The leagues may be sponsored by clubs, by business concerns, by churches, or by the town's recreation department.

This book's whole purpose is to help you find your place in the game, whether you join a team or just get together for a good time with your friends.

In Part One, we'll talk about the basics of soccer—all those skills that enable you to move the ball up and down the field without ever touching it with your hands or arms. These are fun to learn and try for yourself. They range from kicking the ball with either foot to sending it on its way with your head.

Part Two brings us to the game itself. We'll talk about how soccer is played and about the rules that make it such an exciting yet safe sport. Then we'll meet your fellow players, talk about the positions on the team, and study the tactics you use to win games.

In Part Three, we'll try the exercises you can use to develop and perfect your basic skills so that you'll be the best player possible. Next, we'll spend a chapter with some exercises that are special fun—these are really mini-games in themselves and don't require a whole team to play. Finally, we'll put everything together in a personal training program you can follow throughout the year. With it, you'll always be ready to play when soccer season rolls around.

So welcome to soccer and all its fun—and let's get to work.

part one
the basics

2
kicking

There are many different kicks in soccer. Made with various areas of the foot, they are meant to send the ball in any direction desired, and at any speed or height. There are so many kicks, in fact, that once you've learned them all, you'll be greeting the ball with practically every part of your foot.

But numerous though they are, all soccer kicks can be divided into four basic types—the *instep kick*, the *pass*, the *volley*, and the *dribble*.

THE INSTEP KICK

This kick is made with the instep, that broad area across the top of your foot where your shoelaces are. The kick serves so many purposes in a game that it is called the basic soccer-style kick.

Made in one way, the instep kick drives the ball low along or just above the ground to a teammate. Made in another, it sails the ball high into the air and drops it safely far downfield. It can also gently arc the ball over a nearby opponent's head to one of your teammates close behind. Or, if made with an extra burst of power, it can smash the ball so low and hard into the goal that the goalkeeper has little chance to stop it.

The instep kick is both powerful and accurate, because it is made with such a broad area of the foot. It is far more effective than kicking with the toes, a fact that explains its growing popularity as a kickoff and field-goal weapon in American football. The toe kick, though used in soccer at times for distance, generates power but little accuracy. The instep kick gets the most out of each.

This is another reason why it is known as the basic soccer-style kick. The best soccer kicks always use broad areas of the foot. The instep kick teaches the player early on to "get away from the toes."

Now to try it for ourselves, first sending the ball low along the ground. Though the ball will usually be on the move during a game, we'll start with it stationary on the ground.

The Low Instep Kick　Position yourself about ten yards straight behind the ball and plan to hit it at the center panel—the panel that is halfway between the top of the ball and the ground. If you hit the ball any lower, you may go right under it and sail it into the air. If you strike it higher up, you may actually step on top of it.

Looking right at the center panel, run forward and plant your non-kicking foot directly alongside the ball, with your toes pointing straight ahead. Bend your non-kicking leg deeply. Lean forward right over the ball; this will help you to drive it down and keep it low to the ground.

Now for your kicking foot: Swing it up behind you from the knee. Point your toes out to the rear. Next, bring the foot down and forward in a smooth arc. On impact, the upper area of your instep should sink into the center while the curve made by your ankle and toes wraps itself about the ball.

As soon as your foot touches the ball, straighten your leg powerfully. Then follow through all the way, letting the leg rise in front of you and pointing the toes along the path that you want the ball to take. The ball should travel low to the ground, along an arrow-straight course.

Let your arms rise out to the sides as you run to the kick. They are quite naturally working to help keep you in balance.

Throughout the run and the kick, never take your eyes from the ball. You'll miss your target if they drift away for even an instant.

Illustration 2   The *low in-step kick* drives the ball along the ground. In the small picture, you can see how the instep strikes the center panel on the ball. When making this or any other kick, don't cut your follow-through short or your foot may twist at the last second. Then, where the ball will go is anybody's guess.

In fact, no matter what kick you're making, always remember the soccer player's cardinal rule: *Keep your eyes on the ball.*

One last important point: Every good soccer player can kick the ball equally well with either foot. So be sure to try the kick with your "weaker" foot—your left foot if you're right-footed. *All* soccer kicks should be practiced with each foot.

Now here's the kick that lofts the ball high and sends it far downfield.

The Lofted Instep Kick The lofted kick differs from the low kick in three ways. First, you plan to strike the ball lower down, so that your foot will be just slightly beneath it. Second, you plant your non-kicking foot not just to the side of the ball but also slightly *behind* it; this forces your kicking leg into a curving swing that brings your foot under the ball. Finally, at the moment of impact, you lean far back.

Working together, these three differences result in a "scooping" action that lifts the ball into its downfield flight.

All else remains as before. Your knees bend as you enter the kick. Your kicking foot rides up sharply behind you, with the toes pointed to the rear. The foot then comes smoothly through the swing. Your kicking leg, aimed along the path of the ball, rises high in the follow-through. The ball sails far downfield.

But suppose you want to send the ball to a nearby teammate by pitching it just over the head of an opponent who stands between. Try the lofted kick again, but this time do not point your toes down. Instead, drop your heel so that your foot is horizontal to the ground when it hits the ball. The foot will touch the ground, go under the ball, and scoop it almost straight into the air. You can help matters along by turning up your toes in the instant of impact. Be sure to kick the ball softly, just hard enough to send it the required distance and about ten feet high.

This kicking action is called *chipping.* The kick itself is known as the *lob* or the *chip.*

When first learning the lofted and low instep kicks, practice with a stationary ball for several days. You'll be eager to test yourself with a moving ball, but remember that kicking a ball when it is scooting here and there is anything but an easy job. Perfect timing is required to reach the ball and then kick it neither too soon nor too late. Proper timing will come much faster if you first learn the basics of each kick with a stationary ball. And remember to practice with each foot.

Illustration 3   Laura uses the *lofted instep kick* to send the ball sailing high and far downfield. The small picture shows how her foot "scoops" up the ball by coming under it. As she is doing, plant your non-kicking foot to the side of and just behind the ball. Then lean far back to give the ball height. On the follow-through, let your kicking leg rise naturally.

THE PASS

The pass is not actually a way to kick the ball. It is any kick that sends (or, in soccer terms, *passes*) the ball from one teammate to another. Made at any time—perhaps when you're running with the ball at your feet, perhaps when you're standing in place—it is one of the most important soccer arts. And well it should be, for soccer is a team game. No player should ever attempt to hold the ball and dazzle the crowd by scoring every point single-handedly. It should always be passed as soon as possible to a teammate who is better positioned to move it downfield.

All kicks in soccer can serve as passes. The instep kick is an effective pass, as is the volley, which we'll meet in a few moments. But the kicks most frequently used are two that are made off the side of the foot—the *inside-of-the-foot* pass and its *outside-of-the-foot* brother.

The Inside-of-the-Foot Pass Like the instep kick, this pass gives maximum power and accuracy because a large area of the foot meets the ball. You'll find yourself depending on it mostly for passes along the ground for distances of 20 and 25 yards. An extra snap of the leg, though, will send the ball as far as 40 yards.

As usual for your first experiment, a stationary ball should be used. And, as usual, once you've backed off ten yards, take a moment to think of where you plan to strike the ball—again on the center panel so that the ball stays low to the ground.

Begin your run, arms rising comfortably out to your sides for balance. End up by planting your non-kicking foot beside the ball, but a few inches away so that you'll have ample room to swing through the kick. Carry your kicking leg back about 12 inches. . . .

But now, in the very same instant, you must add something new. So that you can strike the ball with the side of your foot, turn your kicking leg out from the hip. And bend the knee a bit so that your foot comes off the ground the necessary two or three inches.

Now bring your kicking leg forward. Contact with the ball should be made alongside the upper lacings on your shoe. On impact, straighten your leg for power. Be sure to follow through.

And don't forget: eyes on the ball the whole time.

Illustration 4   Caroline greets the ball at about its center panel to make sure her *inside-of-the-foot pass* stays on the ground. As in the small picture, contact the ball alongside the upper lacings on your shoe. Follow through, letting your leg swing several inches along the ball's path.

The Outside-of-the-Foot Pass   This pass lacks power and so is best used when the ball is transferred to a teammate quite nearby. It has one great advantage, however. It can be used to deceive an opponent who thinks you are simply running alongside the ball and perhaps trying to position yourself for some other kick. Just deftly flick the ball off to the side—and away goes your teammate with it.

When trying the pass for the first time, start the ball rolling and then run alongside it. When you're ready, bend the knee of your kicking leg slightly, drawing your foot up. At the same time, turn

Illustration 5   Caroline uses the *outside-of-the-foot pass* (her teammate waiting at right is just outside the picture). Caroline's bent leg is
straightening in the follow-through. She strikes the ball at the side of her
shoelaces.

the toes down slightly and a bit inward. Now swing your foot. Aim
to strike the ball near the top of your foot, just to the side of your
upper lacings.

It's a bit difficult, isn't it? You'll need to practice before the
muscles in your foot learn what to do and feel comfortable when

making the kick. But persevere. Like all the kicks in soccer, it's fun to master.

Heel and Sole Passes   Though most passes are made off the side of the foot, your heel or sole may be used to send the ball on its way. Both these methods, of course, are used to drive the ball *behind* you.

For the heel pass, give the ball another roll along the ground. Let it travel a few feet out in front of you before running after it. Then overtake it, step over it with one foot, and punch it to the

Illustration 6   The *heel* and *sole passes* send the ball to a teammate behind you. At left, Michael gets off a nice heel pass with a solid punch. At right, Carlos brings the front of his foot far down over the ball before pushing it to the rear.

rear with your heel. Allow your foot to rise several inches from the ground in the follow-through.

The sole pass must be made when the ball is lying still or almost at a stop. Place your foot on top of the ball. Let your toes angle down to the front, and then push the ball to the rear.

THE VOLLEY

Suppose that you must meet the ball while it is still in the air. Out of your bag of soccer skills comes the volley. With it, you can intercept the ball on the bounce or the fly and send it to a teammate, drive it far downfield, or smack it home for a point.

There are many kinds of volleys, but they all spring from a basic two—the *instep volley* and the *half-volley*. Both are very similar to the ordinary instep kick, the only difference (but what a difference it is!) being that the ball is in the air.

The Instep Volley and Half-Volley   The instep volley is made just before a flying ball hits the ground and is most often used by defenders to clear the ball away from their goal by driving it far downfield. The half-volley is made in the instant after the ball has struck the ground. It comes in handy when a player cannot reach the ball for the instep volley and so must play the ball on the bounce.

For the instep volley, position yourself in the path of the ball. Plant your non-kicking foot firmly on the ground and swing your kicking leg back, bending it at the knee. Now bring it forward in time to meet the ball with your full instep at about knee height. Lean far back at the moment of impact so that the ball is driven skyward. Follow through all the way, going right up on the toes of your standing foot. Let your kicking foot rise high—to eye level if it pleases.

When half-volleying, try to hit the ball as it is bouncing about six to twelve inches off the ground. Hold your body well over the ball and bring your foot through the swing with your toes pointing downward, just as if you are making a low instep kick. Meet the ball with your full instep. Caught a few inches off the ground, the ball will fly downfield.

Illustration 7   **Proper timing is everything for the** *instep volley* **(left) or the** *half-volley.* **If you kick too early or too late, you may send the ball flying aimlessly away. Or worse—you may miss it altogether.**

Other Volleys   There are many ways to volley. Each depends on the direction, speed, and height of the ball. Each, of course, presents its own individual problems, all of which can be solved with practice and playing experience. Illustration 8 shows three volleys seen in every game.

Suppose you're the player in Picture A. The ball is approaching at a point somewhere between your ankles and the top of your knees. You can kick it away with the side of your foot. With the knee well bent, raise your leg until your foot is level with the ball. Then greet the ball with a short but firm swing of about six to nine

Illustration 8   Picture A: The *side-of-the-foot volley*. Picture B: The *high volley* when the ball is off to your side. Picture C: The *low overhead volley*. Also known as the scissors kick, this is one of soccer's most difficult kicks. For safety, practice on a gym mat with a coach or an experienced player helping.

inches, striking the ball just as your leg begins to swing upward. The angle at which you hold your foot and leg will determine the height and direction of the kick.

Now you're the player in Picture B. The ball is coming in just above your knees. Quickly turn your body at an angle to the ball's path, bring up your leg, and swing it almost horizontally through the kicking action. At the same time, turn your foot so that you meet the ball squarely with your full instep. You need not attempt a full, swinging kick. A short, jabbing one is better.

And imagine you're the player in Picture C, making one of the most spectacular kicks in soccer—the overhead volley. Its purpose is to drive the ball low over your head to the rear.

As the ball approaches, you go off the ground with *both* feet, swinging up your kicking foot first and then following with your non-kicking foot. In the same instant, let the top half of your body begin to fall back so that your face will be out of the way when you send the ball whizzing past it. And let your hands, with fingers spread, drop to cushion your coming landing.

Strike the ball when it is at about shoulder height. Hit it with your full instep. You'll need a hard, sharp knee action to give the kick power. Your toes should be pointed back toward your shin to help whip the ball past your head.

This is a difficult kick to make, one that will need much practice before it is perfected. It is also a bit on the dangerous side because it sends your leg flying so high. Your foot can very easily hit someone in the face. So, for the safety of everyone around you, never try the kick when you're playing in crowded quarters. In fact, all high kicks should be avoided when players are quite close by.

Incidentally, you need not throw both feet into the air if you wish to drive the ball *high* back over your head. What is needed here is the lofted instep kick, with the leg swung especially high. If you point your toes back toward your shin and meet the ball when it is about waist high, it will sail to the rear in a high arc. But if the play calls for you to keep the ball *low*, then all the acrobatics seen in Picture C become necessary.

THE DRIBBLE

One of soccer's most basic skills, the dribble is just what it is in basketball, except that it's done with the feet. It is the art of moving the ball along the ground and keeping it away from all opponents until you can pass it to a teammate or try for a goal.

The dribble consists of a series of short, pushing kicks that keep the ball in front of you but always within easy reach. The kicks may be made with either the inside or the outside of the foot. The inside-of-the-foot method is the more popular, for it gives the player greater control over the ball. The outside-of-the-foot method is used most often for speed.

The Inside-of-the-Foot Dribble   Relax a moment and then walk forward, tapping the ball ahead of you from foot to foot as you take normal steps. But turn each foot out slightly so that the large joint behind your big toe strikes the ball and sends it angling out across your path to your opposite foot. And tap *lightly*. You never want to scoot the ball out of reach. As you move, try to give an easy rhythm to the dribble, one that seems to whisper right-tap, left-tap, right-tap, and so on.

On impact, your foot should be raised at least two or three inches, so that the ball will remain on the ground. You help matters by crouching over the ball—if you lean backwards, you'll go under the ball and lift it away and out of control.

It is very important to remain relaxed at all times. Let the knees bend comfortably. Keep the hips loose. Not only will your control of the ball be better but, when an opponent one day looms up ahead in a game, you'll be able to change speed and direction in an instant and without losing your balance.

The Outside-of-the-Foot Dribble   Now just one foot is used to move the ball. Turn that foot in slightly so that it taps the ball near the little toe. As the ball rolls forward, pursue it, turn the foot in again, and once more send the ball on its way.

As always, keep your eyes on the ball and your body crouched forward. Stay relaxed. And practice with both feet.

When you first try the dribble, use a stationary ball. Just stand

Illustration 9 **Carlos keeps the ball away from Mai Wei with the**
inside-of-the-foot dribble. **He uses both feet alternately to move the ball.**
Notice their different heights: players of all sizes enjoy soccer together.

beside it and practice touching it with your little toe. Then dribble
at a slow walk, gradually increasing your speed as you gain confidence. Remember always to tap lightly so that the ball never
scoots too far to your front.

Light taps are so important that they deserve another mention.
One day in a game, whether dribbling with either the inside or the
outside of the foot, you may find yourself in an area pretty free
of opponents. Then it's all right to pick up speed by driving the

Illustration 10   The *outside-of-the-foot dribble* is one of soccer's most difficult kicks because the foot must be turned sharply inward (as if you're pigeon-toed) as you meet the ball. It's good to practice first with a stationary ball, as Sharon is doing. Just touch it again and again with your little toe.

ball a yard or more to your front. At all other times, though, the taps *must* be used to keep the ball within easy reach—"right on the toe," as many players say. It's the only way to protect the ball from all those enemy feet that want to "grab" it.

Obviously, the kick in soccer is equivalent to the throw in football or baseball. And, like the throw, it has an opposite action—the catch or, in soccer terms, the *trap*. The next chapter brings us to that very demanding skill.

3
trapping

When trapping, you "catch" the ball without using your hands or arms. You stop the ball in such a way that it ends up close to the feet, ready to be dribbled, kicked, passed, or shot for a goal. Many parts of the body are used in trapping. But, soccer being what it is, the foot is always the busiest of the "trappers."

In the next pages, we'll be trying all sorts of traps to stop the ball on the ground and in the air. They may be used to receive kicks and passes from a teammate or to intercept the ball as it is traveling from one opponent to another. Each trap requires movements all its own, and each requires that you follow two basic rules.

First, remain alert at all times. Always look for the ball. Always remember that it can—and assuredly will—come at you from *any* direction and at *any* height and speed at *any* time. Never let it surprise you, and never just stand there awaiting its arrival. Move to it as fast as you can. Gauge the spot where the two of you will converge. Then quickly position yourself for the trap.

Second, no matter what part of your body makes the trap, always cushion the ball so it does not bounce away. Should you present an unyielding surface—whether it be your foot, your leg, or your chest—the ball will sail off as if kicked. But if you relax and "give a little"—that is, pull back an inch or so on impact—the ball will behave as though it has hit a mattress. It will drop right at your feet.

Here are the traps most often used in a game. We start with the always-busy foot.

TRAPPING WITH THE FOOT

The good player learns to stop a ball expertly with either foot. The foot chosen for the trap is called the controlling foot, and it should be able to stop the ball in any of four ways—with either side, the sole, or the instep. Each method works well for both ground and airborne balls.

The Inside-of-the-Foot Trap   Here you trap the ball with the same area of the foot used to make the inside-of-the-foot pass—that broad stretch from the base of the big toe back along the length of the arch. Broad as it is, it provides a fine cushion when made to "give" a little.

First, imagine that the ball is rolling on the ground, coming head-on or slightly from the side. Quickly position yourself at about a 45° angle to the approach, so that the sides of your feet are presented to the ball. With a bend of the knee, raise your controlling foot about six or seven inches and hold it there until the ball is rolling past the front of your standing foot.

Now the controlling foot comes down into the path of the ball. At the same time, however, it moves out towards your side so it seems to be running just ahead of the ball. This sideward movement gives the trap its cushioning effect, for the ball is actually rolling against the foot. The foot continues traveling for several inches and finally comes to a halt, stopping the ball.

By the way, you did keep your eyes on the ball throughout the trap, didn't you?

Next, suppose the ball is in the air, flying or bouncing at about knee level. Again, position yourself at a 45° angle, but this time place your standing foot just to the front of the spot where you expect the ball to land. Up goes your controlling foot about six or seven inches; now a new movement must be added.

Just before the ball lands, *lean your controlling leg far over it.* This lean angles the side of your foot downward so that a wedge begins to form between it and the ground. On impact, the ball is deflected to the grass, and your foot follows it down to close the wedge. The ball is snared and ready for play.

Illustration 11   Ian makes an *inside-of-the-foot trap* by angling him-self sideways as a ground ball approaches. In this trap, it's best to keep the controlling foot slightly off the ground so the ball can't hop across it. In his excitement, Ian has lowered his foot almost to the ground.

Illustration 12   Carlos snares a bouncing ball with this *inside-of-the-foot trap.* He brings the knee of his controlling leg far over the ball to deflect it downward. The controlling foot will follow the ball down and trap it against the ground. If he doesn't bring his foot down smoothly, he'll stab the ball—sending it away instead of controlling it.

Of course, your foot "gives" an inch or so before pursuing the ball earthward.

It is all-important that you close the wedge in the instant that the ball strikes the ground. The ball must not be given a single chance to bounce before it is trapped firmly in place. Even the slightest bounce will send it skipping away before your foot can reach it.

The Outside-of-the-Foot Trap   In a game, with the ball coming at you fast, you won't always have time to position yourself for the inside-of-the-foot trap. And so you may need to switch to the outside version.

Illustration 13   In stopping a ground ball with the *outside-of-the-foot trap*, the controlling foot cushions the ball and halts it.

There's the ball now, coming along the ground from your right and streaking directly across your path. Step forward to intercept it. Bend your knee deeply and raise your controlling foot—in this case, your right one—about three inches off the ground. Whack! The ball runs into the area just behind your little toe.

Now you must cushion the impact. To do so, carry your right foot across the front of your left one about three or four inches. The ball will run against it the whole time and finally stop. Then quickly remove your controlling foot so that you're ready for a kick or a dribble.

The action for trapping an airborne ball is quite similar. Plant your standing foot just ahead of the anticipated landing spot. Once you've raised your trapping leg, lean it over the ball so that the side of the foot forms that wedge-like angle to the ground. On impact, let the foot ride a few inches across your front for the cushioning effect and, at the same time, lower it to close the wedge.

Once again, remember to close the wedge smoothly.

Illustration 14 **This *outside-of-the-foot trap* stops an airborne ball. In trapping any ball, bring the ball smoothly to a halt. Don't stab at it.**

The Sole Trap   The sole is as fine a trapper as the sides of the foot. It's especially useful when the ball is whizzing straight at you along the ground or dropping close to your feet.

Whether the ball is rolling or dropping, extend your control-

Illustration 15   In the *sole trap*, stop the ball at a comfortable distance in front of you. If the ball comes too close, it may roll under you. Or, if you reach too far front, you'll stretch your leg uncomfortably. In both cases, you may lose balance, and you'll also lose time getting back into position.

ling leg to it and bring your foot a few inches clear of the ground. Form the usual wedge by angling your sole upward from the heel. When the ball arrives, cover it with the front half of the sole and close the wedge by dropping your heel to the ground. To cushion, just let your foot ride back a little and relax your ankle.

The Instep Trap   The instep trap comes in handy when a ground ball tries to roll past to one side or the other. Simply extend your leg to the ball and turn your instep so that the ball runs into it. The instep trap does its best work, though, when it snares a ball that is dropping from on high.

As the ball is falling, do just what the player in Picture 16A is doing—position yourself so that it will drop right in front of you. Watching the descent all the while, raise your trapping foot about six or seven inches and place it directly in the ball's path. Point your toes straight ahead and keep your foot horizontal to the ground so that the top of the instep is presented fully to the ball.

On impact, relax the foot and let it give way before the ball. But do not give just an inch or so. Rather, as seen in Picture 16B, lower your foot quickly but *steadily* to the ground. The ball will "ride" the instep right to the turf. In the last split second before actually touching the ground, withdraw your foot and prepare for the next play.

TRAPPING WITH THE LEG

The foot may well be the busiest of the trappers, but the leg certainly runs it a close second. Coming into play now are the shin and the thigh. Both are well able to trap the airborne ball when the foot cannot do so.

The Shin Trap   Suppose the ball bounces to you just below knee level. You can make the stop simply by bending your knees forward out over the ball and deflecting it downward with one or both shins. Cushion by relaxing and pulling back slightly on impact.

As soon as the ball touches the ground, you'll realize that the trap is only half completed. Even after dropping such a short

Illustration 16
There are two moves in the *instep trap*. First, Carlos brings his foot up gently to meet the dropping ball with his instep. Then he lets the ball ride on his instep as he lowers his foot to the ground smoothly and steadily.

distance, the ball will bounce and skip away unless quickly held in check. And so you must straighten in a flash and put one foot or the other to work with one of its traps, completing the stop by stifling the bounce.

This "second trap" is always needed when the leg or some area of the upper body deflects the ball to the ground. Practically all of the foot traps that we've mentioned can be used; the most helpful one is the inside-of-the-foot trap.

The Thigh Trap   The thigh is the broad and fleshy area above the knee. It can be used to stop a ball coming in from your front or side.

Let's say that the ball is to your front, bouncing or flying low. Like the player in Picture 17A, bend your trapping leg and bring the knee about halfway up to hip level. Once the knee is in place, the top of the thigh will be facing the ball and sloping downward.

Try to make the trap midway between the knee and the hip. There, where the thigh is broadest and fleshiest, it can best cushion the ball. Help the cushioning by relaxing the thigh on impact. Then immediately pull your leg back and place it alongside your standing leg. The ball will bounce slightly and seem to "run down" the leg to the ground.

But what if the ball is coming down right out of the sky? Now bring your thigh all the way up until it is horizontal to the ground and forms a flat "landing pad" for the ball. As before, relax the thigh on impact, but this time there's no need to straighten the leg. Hitting a soft and relaxed horizontal surface, the ball will hop an inch or so and then roll off the side of the thigh.

Now a last play: This time the ball comes bouncing or flying in from the side. As shown in 17B, you can greet it with the inside of the thigh close to the knee. Pull the knee up high enough to put the thigh in the ball's path, and then give a bit by rotating the thigh outward on impact. The ball will bounce lightly and then land in front of your standing foot.

Illustration 17   Picture A: The *thigh trap* **stops a ball dropping down from above. As the ball touches your thigh, drop your leg straight so the ball falls at your feet. Picture B: The** *inside-of-the-thigh trap.* **Rotate your thigh outward slightly, so the flying ball drops right at your feet.**

TRAPPING WITH THE UPPER BODY

The stomach, the chest, and the head are all used to trap balls that are bouncing or flying somewhere above waist level. Of these three trappers, the most popular is the chest because it offers the broadest landing surface for the ball.

The Chest Trap   The chest trap is made in two different ways. One traps the ball dropping from the sky, while the other gets the ball that is traveling horizontally.

The ball comes down from above in Picture 18A. Step into its path and lean back from the waist—*far* back, so that the chest is fully exposed to the ball. Relax on impact and add to the cushioning by pulling the chest in; this will happen automatically if you'll push your shoulders forward.

The ball will hop perhaps three or four inches and then head for the ground. Straighten yourself immediately. Then lean forward to use a foot catch that will keep the ball from bouncing away when it lands.

In 18B, the ball is sailing horizontally or along a very shallow curve. Again, move into its path, jumping if necessary to bring your chest level with it. Now, however, don't arch backward. Instead, sink your chest in by pushing your shoulders forward, and then lean over the ball so that it will be driven downward. As before, relax and give a little on impact.

When jumping for the chest trap, try to kick your feet high behind you. It's an action that helps you defy gravity. You hang suspended in the air an instant longer and so reduce the chances of starting back down before the ball arrives.

In most games today, girls are allowed to protect themselves by crossing their arms in front of their breasts when chesting the ball. However, to avoid touching the ball illegally, the arms must be crossed tightly and held right against the body, with the hands fisted at the shoulders. Neither the hands nor the arms may come away from the body, and neither may deflect or direct the ball in any way.

The stomach trap, which is most often used for balls flying or bouncing in right at waist level, is made in the same way as the

Illustration 18   Picture A: *Chest Trap*, high ball.
Picture B: *Chest trap*, medium-low ball. Chest traps
cushion the ball so it bounces only a few inches
away, then drops right to your feet. Picture C: Caroline shows the way girls protect themselves in a
chest trap by crossing her arms and holding her fists
against her shoulders.

low chest trap. Move into the path of the ball, lean forward slightly as it arrives, relax and give on impact, and deflect it downward.

The Head Trap One of the most difficult of all "catches" is the head trap. You meet the ball with the center of your forehead just below the hairline, cushioning the impact by relaxing your neck muscles and sinking down deeply on one knee. All this requires very precise timing, and coaches advise that the head trap be tried only by expert players. They suggest that the head be used mostly to "kick" the ball away. We'll be talking about this in the next chapter.

4
rounding out your skills

Dribbling, kicking, and trapping must be joined by *heading*, *tackling*, and *throwing in*. These three final skills round out your soccer abilities and enable you to make your fullest contribution to the team effort.

HEADING

Heading the ball is the art of "kicking" the ball with your head.

Heading is a skill that often sends you leaping acrobatically. It is most frequently used when the ball is flying too high to be stopped by another part of the body or when there isn't time for a trap and a kick. Also, because it is a move that can be made quickly when you're crowding around the goal, it is often used to zip the ball past the goalkeeper and into the net.

For your first experiments, ask a friend to toss the ball to you underhanded so that it rises to your head and can be butted right back and caught. Position yourself in its path. Plant one foot firmly ahead of the other and then keep two thoughts uppermost in mind:

First, plan to meet the ball with the center of your forehead, just below the hairline, where the skull is the sturdiest. Second, never take your eyes off the oncoming ball. You'll blink automatically on impact, but resist every impulse to shut your eyes beforehand. Even a blink can pull you off your target, causing you to meet the ball too low or too high. In either case, it will pop away in some unwanted direction.

As the ball approaches, let your body help your head. Bend

Illustration 19 In *heading*, punch the ball solidly with your forehead. The punch, with your head thrusting forward and your neck muscles stretching, gives the ball power and direction. Don't draw back from the ball—the sturdiest part of your forehead will meet it and your neck muscles will absorb the impact.

your knees. Tilt your upper body back, carrying the head along with it. Then, just before impact, lunge forward right at the ball by straightening your knees and whipping your upper body and head forward. Literally punch the ball with your forehead, stretching the neck muscles as you do so. Then follow through, carrying your head forward along the path that you want the ball to travel.

You may think you'll feel pain when you head the ball. But don't worry too much. If you bring your head forward *correctly*, you'll feel the impact, yes, but no pain as such. For the sturdiest part of your forehead will meet the ball and your neck muscles will absorb the shock.

Once you're used to heading the ball while standing in place, you can try a leap. As your friend throws the ball higher now, run to it and, without breaking stride, plant your front foot and then use it as a springboard. Sail into the air. Arch your head and body back and then snap them forward at the right moment. Your impact area remains the same—the center of the forehead just below the hairline. Punch the ball hard and follow through. Eyes open and on the ball throughout the jump and the follow-through.

It's a good idea always to pull your legs hard up behind you as you did when chesting. They'll help you remain suspended a fraction of a second longer. And, as a bonus, they'll help to arch your upper body strongly back. Then it can come forward all the more powerfully.

Your first practice sessions are best spent heading the ball straight back to your friend. But soon you can begin adding some variations—and very interesting variations they'll prove to be.

For instance, have your friend throw the ball in different directions and at various heights while you dash to it, position yourself, and meet it, sometimes with both feet on the ground and sometimes while leaping. Next, begin to aim the headed ball in various directions as if passing it to various teammates. This is done by first "seeing" where the imaginary teammate is positioned. Then fasten your eyes on the ball and, on impact, thrust your head in the desired direction.

Finally, give much attention to driving the ball high and then low. Like the instep kick, the header sends the ball high and far downfield if made powerfully, or right over the head of an opponent to a teammate just behind if softly made. The low header serves as a pass to the feet of a teammate or as a shot into the goal net.

For the high header, come under the ball and punch its bottom side, hitting the exact spot that will send it along the desired path. At first, you'll likely come too far under and pop the ball straight up. In time, with practice, you'll develop an instinct for finding just the right spot.

Your head must come far forward for the low header, so that the ball is driven downward. This forward thrust is especially necessary in the goal shot, for the ball must fly into the net and not above the crossbar. And the thrust must be powerful if the ball is to be shot past an alert goalkeeper.

One final point: Pay strict attention to your arms when heading. Try to keep them tucked in as close as possible to your sides, especially when you're leaping high in a crowd. Should they fly out wildly and strike an opponent, you'll be assessed a penalty for hitting, shoving, or pushing, all strictly forbidden by the rules of soccer. At the same time, however, do not bring them so high up against you that they'll touch the ball should the header go awry.

TACKLING

So far, we've talked about the basic skills needed to move the ball along the field. All of them are primarily attack weapons, though headers and certain kicks can be used to intercept the ball while you're on defense. With the tackle, however, we come to a purely defensive skill—in fact, to the chief defensive skill in soccer.

The soccer tackle bears no resemblance whatsoever to the tackle in football. In football, you pull the ball carrier to the ground. In soccer, you tackle the ball. You go after the ball and try to kick it away from the dribbler or somehow gain possession of it for yourself. You may also use the tackle to force the dribbler out of bounds so that the play ends.

The tackle is made with the feet. It is subject to many restrictions because soccer is not a rough body-contact game. Just as you are not allowed to touch the ball with your hands or arms, you may not push or strike the dribbler during the tackle. Nor may you roughly block the dribbler, though you can use your shoulder at times. You are also not allowed to jump at or trip the dribbler.

These restrictions are meant to avoid injury. They make tackling one of the most difficult arts and soccer one of the safest games. The restrictions, however, do not mean that tackles can't be made strongly. Actually, strong but clean and careful tackles are the safest. Halfhearted tackles on the one hand, and rough, careless tackles on the other, are the ones that cause injuries.

You can help yourself play within the restrictions and avoid injuries and penalties if you keep three points in mind: (1) Always tackle vigorously and cleanly, (2) always target in on the ball, not the dribbler, and (3) always try to the take the ball when it is rolling free of the dribbler's foot.

The Front Tackle Tackles are made from the front, the side, and the rear. The front tackle is the simplest.

It begins as you plant yourself in the dribbler's path. Spread your feet and crouch forward for balance. Tuck your elbows in against your sides so that there will be no danger of a pushing or shoving penalty.

Your next move depends on what your opponent does. Suppose he or she tries to escape to your right. As in Picture 20A, your right foot goes out to snare the ball. Your body comes forward to get between the dribbler and the ball.

Blocked this way, your opponent goes off balance. The momentum of running begins to pull the dribbler's foot up from the ball. Then, as in 20B, you scoot the ball out from under the rising foot and take over for a dribble or a kick.

Many times, however, the dribbler will not go off balance and will be able to lodge the kicking foot firmly against the ball. You may then find the ball stuck between the two of you. Instantly— but smoothly—run your foot under the ball and flick it free across the dribbler's toes.

When tackling from the front, you are especially vulnerable to feints, all those moves that are meant to fake you into thinking that the dribbler intends to move in one direction when a dash in the opposite direction is really planned. To protect yourself, always keep your eyes on the ball. False moves by an opponent's shoulders, head, and eyes can always fool you. But the ball can't. Watching it, you'll see exactly where it's being taken.

Side Tackles An action similar to the front tackle can be used to grab the ball from the side or the rear. Move in close and then send your foot out to snare the ball when it is rolling free of the dribbler's foot. But take care, for the tackle can be extremely dangerous. All too easily, you can trip and perhaps injure the

Illustration 20 *Tackling*. **Picture A: Caroline tackles the ball as it leaves Carlos' dribbling foot. Picture B: Another time, as the momentum of running brings Carlos' foot off the ground, Caroline slips the ball beneath his raised foot.**

dribbler—and most certainly be assessed a penalty. A tackle of this sort, whether made from the side or the rear, should be saved for that day when you're an expert player.

The most basic side tackle is the *shoulder charge.* It permits a shoulder nudge or brush that veers the dribbler away from the ball so that you can take charge.

To make the tackle, first run right alongside the dribbler. Next, dropping your shoulder slightly, move in and nudge the dribbler off course. Then go for the ball, taking it under immediate control.

No part of the body other than the shoulder may touch the dribbler during the tackle. So be sure to keep your arms close to your sides so your elbows are safely out of the play. Watch out, too, that your hip doesn't bounce out to do damage. And, no matter the heat of the game, never lose your head and do more than nudge or brush the dribbler aside. An unduly rough or violent shoulder charge is a sure penalty.

One of the most exciting side tackles is the *sliding tackle*. It is often made when a dribbler across the field from you has broken free of most of your teammates and is running deep into your territory. You must dash in pursuit and then slide across the dribbler's path and into the ball. Your aim now is not to take control of the ball but simply to kick it away, perhaps out of

Illustration 21   The *shoulder charge* forces the dribbler away from the ball. Michael (left) takes the ball from Caroline. He keeps his left elbow tucked in to avoid hitting her.

bounds so that the play will be stopped and the scoring attempt spoiled.

The ball is best struck with the foot on the side of your body farthest away from the dribbler.

Suppose that you're coming in from your opponent's right and so must use your right foot. While the ball is rolling free of the dribbler, slide down on your left hip, just as if you were a baseball player coming into second base on a close play. Curl your left leg under you and reach for the ball with your right. Cushion your slide with the palm of your left hand. Stretch your right leg and foot out as far as you can, kicking the ball with either your instep or your toes, preferably the toes because they give an inch or so of extra reach.

There is always the danger of tripping the dribbler during the slide. But the rules say that a penalty will be called only if you trip the dribbler before his or her kick or if you miss the ball altogether. Should the trip occur after the kick, there will be no penalty, for, once the ball is away, it's the dribbler who is responsible for avoiding your legs.

So be sure to time the slide perfectly. Avoid coming any closer than necessary to the dribbler. And, before you ever start down on your hip, be sure that you'll be able to reach the ball.

Though your aim is simply to kick the ball away, many experienced tacklers are able to keep it in their possession by ending the slide with a different action. Rather than striking the ball away, they hook the instep around it and bring it to a stop, holding it in place while the momentum of running carries the dribbler forward another step or two. Once the dribbler is safely away, the tackler swivels about, jumps to his or her feet, and takes full control of the ball.

The tackle, due to the "hooking" action of the instep, is usually called the *hook tackle*. You'll also hear it called the *sliding block tackle*.

Practice will be needed to master the two sliding tackles. Both, of course, demand perfect timing. And both call for a full leg extension that will come only with continued exercise. The full leg extension is a must, because if you fail to reach out far enough to

Illustration 22 For the *sliding tackle*, go after the ball when it's free of the dribbler's feet.

hook the ball or kick it solidly, it will bounce just a few feet away. Then, before you can jump back to your feet, the dribbler will be able to retrieve the ball and head again for the goal.

So you have your work cut out for you. In the beginning try to limit yourself to the simpler tackles during a game. At first, rather than attempting a regular tackle, you might try to force the dribbler over to a sideline so that the ball goes out of bounds. As long as you obey the rules of tackling and do not force the dribbler over roughly, it is a perfectly legal maneuver.

THROWING IN

The last of the basic skills is one that has been called a "soccer oddity"—because it permits the use of hands and arms.

The throw-in is used to start the action again after the ball has gone out of bounds across one of the sidelines. A player on the team that was not the last to touch the ball before play ended stands at the edge of the field and throws to a teammate. (The throw-in is not used, however, when the ball goes over a goal line without entering the goal itself. Two special kicks talked about in the next chapter take its place.)

Though a simple action, the throw-in must be made in a certain way. The ball must be held in both hands and thrown over the head from behind. Both feet must be on or outside the sideline. Part of each foot must remain on the ground throughout the throw. And the ball must go to a teammate and never into the goal for a score. If any of these rules is violated, the ball is given to the opposition for a throw-in.

You may throw the ball a short or long distance. When throwing short, it's usual to stand with your feet together.

Ready yourself by spreading your fingers wide so that they form a basket for the ball. Let the thumbs almost meet at the back of the ball. The throw-in is actually a catapulting action, and the basket helps to fling the ball on its way.

Now hold the ball behind your head. Bend your knees and arch your back. Then, all in one motion, straighten yourself and whip the ball up and forward.

Release the ball just after it passes the top of your head. Finish things off by following through all the way. Let your arms, fully extended, ride out far to your front and along the path of the ball.

The long throw-in is made in the same way, except that you add power by taking a step forward as you fling the ball. Before very long throws, you may take two steps. Be sure, however, that your steps never carry you across the sideline and onto the field.

Momentum may carry you up on your toes during the long throw-in and the follow-through. That's all right, providing that you don't raise either foot completely clear of the ground. After stepping forward on a long throw-in, you may wish to drag the toe of your back foot along the ground until your feet are back together again; many players find that this move helps them to

Illustration 23   Joe sends the ball into play with the *throw-in*. Picture A: Both feet stay together for a short throw-in. Picture B: He steps forward to add power to a long throw-in. The toes of his right foot stay on the ground, even though he leans forward to follow through.

keep their balance. Fine again. Just be sure that the toe is always dragging on the ground.

The throw-in ends our work on the basic skills. Now it's time to turn to the soccer game itself.

part two
game time

5
the rules

Soccer players are very lucky. The rules of the game are among the easiest in sports to understand and learn.

While in football you must memorize more than seventy-five rules, for soccer you need learn only seventeen. Known as "the laws of the game," they apply wherever soccer is found in the world and whether it is played by women or men, or boys or girls.

THE FIELD

A soccer field, sometimes called a *pitch*, is rectangular. The rules permit it to vary in size so that it will fit players of all ages. For older players, the field may measure up to 130 yards long and 100 yards wide. It can be cut down, however, to 100 yards long and 50 yards wide (about the size of a football field) for younger players.

The field is enclosed within four white lines. Two run down the sides and are called the *touchlines* or, as they're called in football, the *sidelines*. Joining them at right angles at either end of the field are the *goal lines*.

Other white lines divide the field into various areas. All the areas are shown in Illustration 24. We'll see the parts they play in a game as we go along.

THE BALL

A soccer ball is about the size of a volleyball. It must be made

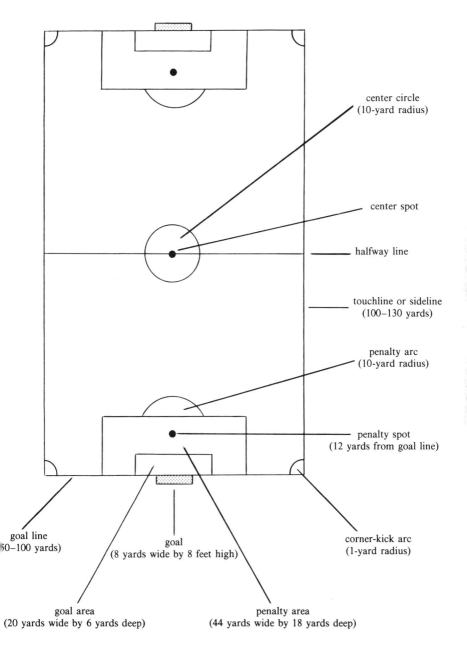

center circle
(10-yard radius)

center spot

halfway line

touchline or sideline
(100–130 yards)

penalty arc
(10-yard radius)

penalty spot
(12 yards from goal line)

goal line
50–100 yards)

goal
(8 yards wide by 8 feet high)

corner-kick arc
(1-yard radius)

goal area
(20 yards wide by 6 yards deep)

penalty area
(44 yards wide by 18 yards deep)

Illustration 24   *The Soccer Field*

of leather or some other material (plastic or rubber) not dangerous to the players. Traditionally, the ball used in a game is supplied by the home team.

The covering of the ball is quite distinctive. It consists of a series of five-sided panels that make up a sphere when joined together. So that the ball can be easily seen by the players and the spectators, the panels are of two sharply contrasting colors. The usual colors are black and white, but it is quite all right to paint a ball with a team's colors—perhaps black and gold, perhaps red and white.

THE OFFICIALS

Every soccer game is supervised by three officials—a *referee* and two *linesmen.* The referee is the leader.

The referee is in complete charge of the game. He enforces the rules, serves as timekeeper, and maintains a record of the game's progress. He has the power to stop the action at any time, perhaps to levy a penalty for some infraction, perhaps to see that an injured player is cared for, or perhaps to caution a player for misbehavior. The referee may even terminate the game if he sees fit. He might do so if bad weather or the rowdy conduct of the teams or the spectators makes further play impossible.

All people on the field are under the referee's control. No one may enter the field without his signal to do so, and he permits no incoming player to leave the sidelines until play has been stopped. Nor does he allow coaches or players to "coach from the sidelines." All substitutions must be reported to him.

The two linesmen stand just outside the touchlines, one to each touchline. Their primary jobs are to signal exactly where the ball goes out of bounds and to indicate which team is to return it to play. They also assist the referee in controlling the game and may call infractions to his attention.

The linesmen carry flags for signaling to the spectators when the ball goes out of play. The flags are usually supplied by the home team. If flags are not available, the linesmen signal with a raised arm.

PLAYER EQUIPMENT

As in any team game, the uniforms worn by all team members should match in color. The colors, of course, should contrast sharply with those of the opposition. Often, the teammates will wear jerseys of one color and shorts of another, with their stockings then combining the two colors.

The goalkeeper, however, wears a uniform different from the regular team outfit. It must stand out clearly so that the goalie is never mistaken for another player when the action sweeps in around the net (we'll see why soon). The goalie often wears shorts the same color as the rest of the team, but always a jersey of a different and easily seen color. The most popular colors for the jersey are black, red, or green, though any color that contrasts with that of the other team shirts is permissible.

The rules state that everything worn by a player must be safe, not only for the player but for everyone else. Wristwatches, bracelets, heavy rings, necklaces, and earrings should never be worn. They all can knick, scratch, or gouge. And necklaces have been known to fly up into someone's face and painfully sting an eye during a sudden twist or whirl.

Shoes are potentially the most dangerous items of player equipment. The rules are quite strict about their safety features. You may wear soccer shoes that have studs or bars on their soles for traction, but you will not be permitted on the field with shoes equipped with cleats, nails, or pegs. The referee checks all shoes before the game and has the right to keep a player off the field until proper and safe shoes are put on.

So that they will be safe, the studs and bars on soccer shoes must be made of certain materials and be of a certain size. If you buy soccer shoes, you don't need to worry about meeting all safety standards. Every American manufacturer makes its soccer shoes according to strict specifications. If you don't buy soccer shoes, you'll be perfectly safe in sneakers.

THE GAME

Though soccer is usually played by two teams of not more than eleven players each, games can be played with as few as seven members per team. There may be two to five substitutions per game. Of course, that number can be increased in informal games so that everyone has the chance to get in on the fun.

Duration of the Game   A regulation game lasts 90 minutes and is divided into two periods of 45 minutes each. Play for young people, however, can be divided into two 30- or 35-minute halves. Some young people's leagues play games of four quarters of 10 to 15 minutes each.

There is an intermission of 5 to 15 minutes at halftime.

Captain's Choice   Just before play begins, the team captains meet on the field for the toss of a coin. The captain who wins the toss is allowed to choose to kick off *or* defend a particular goal.

Should the captain choose to kick off, the opposition will be entitled to kick off at the start of the second half. But should the choice be to defend, say, the northern goal during the first half, then the opposing team will defend that goal during the second half.

The Kickoff   To start the game, the referee places the ball on the center spot. A player on the team kicking off then sends it flying or rolling to a teammate. At the time of the kickoff, each team must be in its half of the field. Further, all opposing players must be at least 10 yards away from the kicker. Here, we see the reason for the center circle, which has a radius of 10 yards around the center spot. Simply by standing outside the circle, the opposing players nearest the kicker know that they are positioned at the required distance.

The kick may be fired to a teammate nearby or to one in the distance. The kicker must be sure to send the ball at least the distance of its own circumference; otherwise it is not considered in play and the kickoff will have to be taken again. Once the ball is on its way, the kicker may not play it again until it touches or is played by another player—either a teammate or someone on the opposing side. If the kicker plays the ball too soon, the team will be penalized. (Special kicks are used for penalties. More about them later.) Also, the kicker may not attempt to score a goal with the kickoff.

The kickoff is used again to start each new period. It also restarts the action after a goal has been scored; the team that was scored against does the kicking.

The kickoff, however, is not used to restart the game when a time-out is called while the ball is still inside the playing field. Rather, as shown in Illustration 25, the referee turns to the *drop*.

If the time-out is called just after the ball has crossed a touch-line, a throw-in returns it to action. Should the time-out come just after the ball goes over a goal line without actually entering the goal itself, one of two kicks we'll talk about later is used.

Illustration 25   The *drop* is similar to the tip-off in basketball. The referee has just dropped the ball. Both players now try to snare it and send it to a teammate.

Handballing   As you know, a player may move the ball with any part of the body except the hands and arms. Only in two instances do the rules permit the ball to be touched or moved by the hands or arms—actions that are called *handballing*. First, there is the throw-in. Second, the goalkeeper may use his or her arms and hands to prevent a score when the ball comes whizzing towards the net. Practically all goal shots are made from close by and would be impossible to stop if the goalie couldn't use the hands and arms. The attackers would then always have an unfair advantage.

All this is the reason for the goalkeeper's distinctive uniform. When the action crowds in on the net, the referee must always be able to see that only the goalkeeper touches the ball. But for that distinctive uniform, any player might be confused with the goalie and be able to break, accidentally or deliberately, one of soccer's basic rules.

The Corner and Goal Kicks   When the ball goes out of bounds across the goal line without entering the goal net, either of two kicks return it to play. These are the *corner* and *goal* kicks.

Suppose your team moves into the opposition's penalty area. You drive the ball in hard for a score, but the goalkeeper or some other opposing player strikes it away, sending it out of bounds over the crossbar or to the side of a goalpost. Since a defender was the last player to touch the ball, your team is entitled to return it to play with the corner kick.

The referee places the ball on the ground within the arc at the corner of the field nearest the spot where the ball went out of bounds. From there, someone on your team kicks it back into play while your opponents hang back at least ten yards from the kicker. The kicker may not play the ball again until another player has touched or played it.

The corner kick is one of the most exciting plays in the game. Why? First, the ball is close to your opponent's goal and so becomes the object of much hard and crowded play when it is kicked. But even more important, the kick itself can score a goal, something that the goal kick, the kickoff, and the throw-in can't do.

Now suppose that one of *your* teammates is the last player to touch the ball before it scoots out of bounds over the goal line. The ball is handed over to a defending player—usually the goalie—who returns it to play with the goal kick.

The goal kick is made from the half of the goal area closest to the spot where the ball went out of bounds. The ball is placed on the ground and then kicked clear out of the penalty area. The kicker must not play the ball again until it has touched or been played by another player. All opposing players are required to stand outside the penalty area until the kick is made. A goal cannot be scored directly from a goal kick.

PENALTIES AND FOULS

What happens when a player, in the heat of play, commits a foul? Since the field does not have the yard markers of football, a loss of yardage cannot be assessed. And so, instead, the ball goes to the opposing team for one of three special kicks—the *indirect free kick*, the *direct free kick*, or the *penalty kick.*

Indirect and Direct Free Kicks　Both the indirect and direct free kicks are taken from the place where the foul happened. The first is awarded for minor fouls, while the latter is reserved for more serious ones. A goal cannot be scored with the indirect free kick, but the direct free kick can be driven into the net for a point.

Both kicks are made in the same way. The ball is placed on the ground. All opposing players are stationed ten yards away. Once kicked, the ball must move the distance of its own circumference before being in play. And it may not be played again by the kicker until it touches or is played by someone else.

There are, however, two extra points that need to be kept in mind about the kicks.

First, if you make either kick from within your own penalty area, all opposing players must stand not only ten yards away but also outside the penalty area until the ball is in play. The ball then must travel clear of the penalty area. If it fails to do so, it must be rekicked.

Second, suppose you're making the kick quite close to the opposition's penalty area. Now your opponents may stand closer in than 10 yards, *providing* they are right on their own goal line between the goalposts.

The Penalty Kick   What happens when the defenders commit a foul within their own penalty area? The always exciting penalty kick now comes into play.

The referee places the ball on the penalty spot. All players leave the penalty area except the kicker and the defending goalkeeper. The kicker is given one chance to drive the ball into the net for a point, while the goalkeeper, who must stand right on the goal line between the goalposts and not move until the kick is made, does everything possible to keep the ball out of the net.

The players outside the penalty area must stand at least ten yards away from the ball. They may not re-enter the area until the ball is kicked. If a player on the kicking team does so, the kick will be disallowed and taken again, even if the ball went into the net for a point. If a defending player is at fault, an indirect free kick will be awarded to the kicking team at the point of the infraction.

Remember that arc at the front edge of the penalty area? It is 10 yards deep and, by standing just beyond it, all players behind the kicker are sure of being the required distance away.

The kicker must drive the ball forward to the net. It is strictly forbidden to try kicking it to a teammate who then tries to slip it past the goalie for a point. As usual, the kicker may not play the ball again until it touches or is played by another player.

Penalties—Direct Free Kick   Nine fouls result in a direct free kick. The opposing team is awarded the kick when you: (1) kick or try to kick an opponent; (2) trip or try to trip an opponent; (3) strike or try to strike an opponent; (4) push an opponent with your hands or arms; (5) hold an opponent with your hands or arms; (6) charge an opponent violently; (7) charge an opponent from behind unless the opponent is *obstructing*—that is, standing between you and the ball; (8) jump an opponent; or (9) strike, touch, or move the ball in any way with your hands or arms.

Penalties—Indirect Free Kick   The indirect free kick is given for any of seven fouls. You are penalized for: (1) playing in a manner considered dangerous by the referee; (2) charging an opponent with your shoulder when the ball is not within playing distance or when the opponent is really not playing it; (3) intentionally obstructing an opponent—coming between the player and the ball—when you are not actually playing the ball; and (4) charging the goalkeeper except when the goalie is holding the ball or obstructing one of your teammates, or has moved out of the goal area.

An indirect free kick is also called when the goalkeeper takes more than four steps while holding or bouncing the ball, throws the ball into the air and catches it again without sending it to another player, or engages in tactics designed to waste time and "eat up the clock."

Finally, the penalty is called when a player is declared *offside.*

Offside   In general, you'll be called offside if you are running ahead of the ball at the moment a teammate passes it to you. The penalty, however, is never called unless you are in your opponents' half of the field and have fewer than two defenders ahead of you; one of those defenders may be the goalkeeper. Finally, the penalty is not called if you dash ahead of the kicker *after* the ball has been passed. What counts is that you not be running ahead of the kicker before and in the split second that the kick is made.

REFEREE CAUTIONS

Here, now, a final word on penalties: Without actually imposing a penalty, the referee may caution a player against playing roughly, using abusive language, or coming close to breaking the rules. If the poor behavior continues or a more serious offense takes place, the referee has the right to make the player leave the game. Play is stopped while the player leaves the field. (He or she is not replaced.) Play begins again with an indirect free kick by the opposing team at the spot where the final trouble occurred.

6
the team

"Where shall I play on the team?"

This is a question for every beginning player. Of course, you should aim for the position you're best suited for, both physically and mentally. To find that spot, you'll need to ask yourself some more questions and answer them as honestly as possible:

"Am I a fast, medium, or slow runner?"

"Am I a lightweight or on the heavy side?"

"Which are the very best of my soccer skills—dribbling, kicking, passing, trapping, heading, or tackling?"

"Do I prefer to be on the attack during a game or am I really happier in a defensive spot, even though I may never have the chance to score a point?"

Honest answers will take you halfway to where you belong. The rest of your job will be to learn what each position does for the team and then find the one that best matches you and your abilities.

The whole purpose of this chapter is to help you make the right match.

TEAM POSITIONS

Today, the positions on a soccer team are known by two different sets of names. The set your team uses will depend entirely on your coach. Some coaches refer to the positions as *fullbacks*, *halfbacks*, *forwards*, and the *goalkeeper*. Others divide them into *back defenders*, *midfielders*, *strikers*, and the goalkeeper.

All this sometimes confuses the beginning player. But there is no reason why the names should bother you, for each set merely says the same thing as the other, but in its own way. Fullbacks are the same as back defenders; halfbacks are the same as midfielders; and forwards are the same as strikers.

The first set of names is older and is still used by most teams. The second set, however, has come into popularity because many coaches feel that the terms back defender, midfielder, and striker better indicate the type of work done by each position, and the part of the field in which each spends the most time. Some soccer experts believe that the second set will completely replace the first in a few years' time.

The positions are divided among the players as the coach sees fit. Then the players are arranged on the field in any formation that the coach feels will provide the best chance for good attack and defense. Throughout its history, soccer formations have been—and still are—many. One of today's most popular formations is shown in Illustration 26.

The 4–3–3 formation is named, as usual, for the number of players in each position. The numbers start with the fullbacks or back defenders, then move upfield (towards the halfway line). The goalkeeper's position is not included in the numbers because the goalie always plays in the same place.

Where do you belong in the formation? You can find out by imagining yourself in each position.

Back Defender/Fullback In this position, stationed close in front of your own goal, you are primarily a defensive player. You plunge forward to meet and stop any attacks driving deep into your territory. If the ball gets past you, only the lone goalkeeper stands between the opposition and a score.

It is vital that you be able to "read" an attacking play quickly so you can move in a flash to intercept a pass or tackle the ball away. You constantly work against heavy odds, for the charging attackers have a momentum that can easily roll right over you. Further, they often send two players against you, one to handle the ball, the other to hold you back. In all, you need a combination

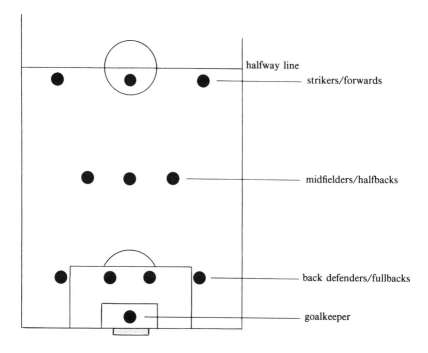

halfway line

strikers/forwards

midfielders/halfbacks

back defenders/fullbacks

goalkeeper

Illustration 26   *The 4–3–3 Formation*

of intelligence, agility, and good physical strength to turn an attack aside and capture the ball.

Once you've got the ball, your job is to drive it far upfield and out of danger. You rarely do this by dribbling and passing. Instead, you depend on the kick and the header. Both must be powerful and accurate, carrying the ball not only to safety but to a teammate who can then start it towards the opposition's goal.

As a back defender, you need at least two additional skills. You have to get away from the carefully developed habit of always keeping your eye on the ball. You do a better job now if you watch the oncoming attackers rather than the ball, so you can see how the attack is taking shape. The back defender who constantly watches the ball always gives some attacker the chance to sneak past or move into a better playing position.

However, once the opponent right in front of you has the ball, then it's eyes on the ball as usual.

You are also called on at times to play the *sweeper* spot. Here, you hover behind your fellow back defenders and then "sweep" to either side, running to any spot where the ball breaks through or where a teammate needs help. You need a sharp eye to see the trouble spots, and quick reflexes if you are to get to them in time.

Midfielder/Halfback Ranging over the field from your own penalty area to—and often beyond—the halfway line, you have two jobs. Part of your time is spent on offense, part on defense.

On offense, you serve as a link between the back defenders and the strikers, receiving the ball from the backs and then passing and maneuvering it along the field until it can be given to the strikers for its final journey to the goal. Because of this "connecting" function, you and your fellow midfielders are often called *linkmen*.

On defense, you may be assigned to guard against an opposing striker, or you may be responsible for a particular area or zone. The choice is up to your coach. In either case, you quickly intercept any attack coming your way, capture the ball, and then instantly decide how best to move it to a position where a scoring attempt into enemy territory can be made by the strikers.

Your abilities are many. On defense, you tackle strongly and expertly. On offense, your passes are always accurate. At all times, you have speed and stamina to spare, because you're always moving at a run when the ball is in your part of the field. Your reactions are fast, so you can always follow and get to the ball. And, because the ball can change possession so often around midfield, you become a top player when you develop a special sixth sense that helps you anticipate when and where each change will take place.

Striker/Forward As the first of the two names indicates, you are a member of the unit that strikes the ball home, into the net for a score. Your unit does the work of receiving the ball from the midfielders and then takes it deep into enemy territory, developing a final scoring attack as you go.

You are a determined and agile player. Determination drives you relentlessly towards the goal, no matter the defenders in your way. Agility is a must, for unless you can scoot or twist away from the defenders, you're not going to keep the ball long.

Your skills? They depend a lot on where you play in the unit.

Let's say you're positioned on the outside, near one of the touchlines. You are called an *outside striker*, an *outside forward*, or a *winger*. Speed and the ability to dribble are your chief assets—without them, you can never streak past the charging defenders. You also pass accurately, with the *wall pass* as one of your specialties. The wall pass, made as a tackler closes in, sends the ball to a teammate who instantly kicks it back—but to a spot that you've reached behind the tackler. The ball behaves just as if you've bounced it off a wall. The pass is also sometimes called *give-and-go*.

Another of your specialties is the *cross* or *crossing pass*. Very often, to outdistance a defender, you dribble fast down the sidelines to the corner of the field. Then suddenly you kick the ball across the field to a fellow striker positioned near the goal. The kick is made in the same way as a lofted instep kick, except that, as your kicking foot meets the ball, you pivot hard on your non-kicking foot, turning in the direction that you want the ball to travel. The kick, which can also be used by other players in other parts of the field, generates tremendous power.

Still another of your specialties is the corner kick, a job most often assigned to the outside forwards. Again, the pivot kick is a fine weapon, made this time with the ball stationary on the ground. You often aim for a spot six to eight feet in front of the goal. There, a fellow striker receives the ball and attempts to drive it home with a kick or a header.

As a winger, you are also well able to head the ball past the goalkeeper or chip it over a defender's head, sending it into the net itself or to a fellow striker positioned for a scoring shot.

But suppose you're stationed in the middle of the unit. You are called an *inside striker* or an *inside forward*. Positioned deep in from the sidelines, you advance along a pretty straight line to the center of the goal and are usually in a better spot for a scoring try than the wingers are.

Because of this special placement, one of the inside strikers is usually assigned the chief responsibility for making goals. If that job is yours, you are the *central striker* or the *center forward.* Your fellow strikers always do what they can to maneuver the ball so that you can drive it home. All strikers are good kickers and headers. As central striker, you must be the best of the lot, able to kick and head powerfully and with unerring accuracy. Both feet must be able to kick with equal ability.

No matter where you play in the striking unit, your coach always insists that you make short passes, for they run far less risk of interception in close quarters. And the coach works you steadily until you are exceptionally good at *screening* the ball. Screening is a pivoting move that quickly puts your body between an opponent and the ball. It may be used anywhere on the field, but it becomes especially important in the crowded area around the goal where one tackler after another seems to be right on top of you.

The screen begins when, using the side of your foot, you flick the ball off to your side, in a direction away from a looming tackler. You then turn and follow the ball by swinging about on your non-kicking foot. The whole action ends with the ball again in front of your feet and the frustrated defender safely behind you.

Every striker also plays a defensive role. If you're an inside striker, you usually cover the inside midfielders when the opposition sweeps into your territory. If playing a winger position, you patrol the sidelines protectively and then drop back to help the back defenders.

The Goalkeeper   You are the last defender between the opposition and a score. From your station in the mouth of the goal, you move wherever necessary to meet and ruin scoring shots coming from any direction, and at any height and speed. Sometimes you must leap for them, sometimes kneel, and sometimes dive headlong.

Your job requires many talents. First, you have the physical strength to withstand one hard-driven ball after another for an entire 90 minutes of play. Next, the courage to go after any ball, even if you must dive among thrashing legs and feet to do so. Then the agility and speed to get to the ball in time, no matter where it is. And, finally, a good eye to see where trouble is coming from in the first place.

You are, of course, the only player allowed to use your hands and arms when playing the ball. If you weren't able to do so, practically all goal stops would be impossible, and the attackers would always have an unfair advantage. And so you've developed a set of skills unusual in soccer. You've mastered the ways in which various scoring shots are best caught or deflected with the hands as well as with any other part of the body.

To prepare for any catch or deflection, you enter the goal-

Illustration 27   **Mai Wei in the *goalkeeper's stance*.**

keeper's traditional stance. Setting yourself right in the center of the goal mouth and about a foot out from the goal line, you spread your feet comfortably apart. Your knees bend. Your hands, with fingers spread, rise to your front. You crouch forward. In all, you put yourself into fine balance, ready to spring in any direction, and ready to bring your hands into the path of the ball without a moment's loss.

You have a motto for all catches: "Never let the ball get behind me and never let it rebound to the attackers." And so, at all times, you put as much of your body as possible into the path of the ball. If you make the catch, you immediately hug the ball close to prevent the bounce back to enemy feet. If the catch proves impossible, you try to bat the ball away, either sending it out of bounds or to a spot safely beyond the reach of the opposition.

Ground balls coming straight at you are the easiest to handle. But you don't bend over to grab them, for then they can all too easily slip past between your legs. Rather, as in Illustration 28, you go down on one knee.

As you kneel, you set yourself at a slight angle to the ball so that your legs will "back up" your hands in the event of a bobble. The knee on the ground forms a barrier behind your hands, while the other leg forms a second barrier, this one across the path of the ball. The upthrust leg is well bent so that its foot is close to your opposite thigh. No gap is left between your legs. The ball has no chance to sneak through.

Down go your hands to the ball. You gather it up, letting it roll up your arms and then clasping it tightly against your chest. You're back on your feet in an instant, ready to send the ball to a nearby teammate or safely far downfield. As you rise, you set your feet apart and lean forward to keep from being knocked back into the goal in case you collide with an opponent. If you stumble back over the goal line with the ball, you score a point—for the opposition.

Balls whizzing in at stomach or chest level are gathered in just as tightly. On impact, your shoulders come forward to "cup" your upper body protectively about the ball. Your feet are well spread and your body bent forward, this time not only to keep you

Illustration 28   **Goalkeeper Rob's legs form a barrier, keeping the ground ball from slipping past. The player trying to make Rob miss the catch must stop this once Rob has the ball.**

balanced against a collision but against the force of the arriving ball as well.

Balls coming in high send you leaping above the surrounding players. You time your jumps perfectly, catching the ball with both hands right at the top of the jump. Your hands, with fingers spread, make the catch toward the back of the ball so that it has little chance to slip through and into the net. All in one movement, you bring the ball down and against your chest. As you jump, you're allowed to bring one knee slightly up and forward as a safeguard against charging opponents.

If a high-flying ball is not safely within reach—or is traveling too fast to be handled—you don't attempt to catch it. Rather, as in Illustration 29, you bat it straight back over the crossbar and out of play. Or you deflect it back and to the side so that it goes out of bounds by sailing past one of the goalposts. Or hit it to your front above the heads of the attackers to a teammate.

You always bat the ball away as hard as you can, using one or both hands as need be. Your hands are open or fisted. If fisted, you punch the ball with the side of your hand or the knuckles. You usually save the fists until you are an expert player, for they are a much smaller "bat" than the open hand. On a mistimed jump,

Illustration 29   The ball can't be caught safely, so the goalie tries to bat it over the crossbar. Rob has just started to leap. Next, he'll hit the ball with the front of his fingers.

they can miss the ball altogether or just graze it so it sails weakly off in some unwanted direction.

When batting the ball over the crossbar, you face one great danger. A poorly timed jump or a weak hit can send the ball against the crossbar—and right back to the attackers. So you put all you've got into your every jump. You reach high for the ball, turn your hand in behind it, and then hit with a solid and upward-pushing movement.

Your most spectacular catch is the dive for a ball off to your side. You throw yourself out to your full length, with arms outstretched beyond your head. As soon as you have the ball, you pull it to you, cradle it against your chest, and jump back to your feet.

A skillful dive is an essential tool in your goalkeeper's bag of tricks. You use it against scoring attacks and also against the penalty kick. When that driving, bulletlike kick is made, you can be sure it will be aimed at one corner or another deep in the net. Consequently, you practice the dive until it is perfect, at first using a gym mat for protection. You learn to kick your legs upward as you fly so that some part of your upper body lands first. When your shoulder, your arm, or your hands touch the ground first, you can cradle the ball much more quickly.

You're permitted to throw the ball back into play once you've caught it, sending it to a teammate (most often, you'll aim for a fast outside striker who has come to help your back defenders). The throw is made with a whipping motion similar to that used to send baseballs in from the outfield. The ball, with your hand cupping it at the rear, is carried back behind your shoulder and then is shot forward in one smooth but energetic motion that ends with your arm stretching out along the path of the ball's flight.

Knowing the constant threat of interceptions, you always throw hard and fairly low. Lobs are saved for those times when you have to clear the head of an opponent standing between you and your target.

At times, you fool the opposition by quickly rolling the ball to a nearby teammate. At others, when your targets are all well guarded, you drive the ball far downfield with a punt. It is the same punt used in football, and it sends the soccer ball quite as

Illustration 30 The *diving save* can be hard on a goalie. Long practice is needed to do it right.

Illustration 31 Make the *goalkeeper's throw* in much the same way as you throw a baseball in from the outfield.

far—for distances up to 50 and 60 yards when a truly strong foot is behind it.

In addition to all your special skills, you own one of the busiest voices on the field. Working behind your back defenders, you constantly shout to them, warning them of where you are, so that the danger of collisions is reduced. And because you always have the best overall view of what is happening, you are the "field general" in your area, much as the catcher is in baseball. You shout encouragements, order your teammates to better defensive positions, and warn of all the dangers you see taking shape.

Then, in common with all good leaders, you try to play harder than any of your teammates. Only with the hardest play do you truly inspire and do you fully serve as your team's "last line of defense."

Perhaps these pages have helped you to find the position meant for you. Perhaps you'll need some help from your coach in making your final selection. Or perhaps the coach, needing you in a certain spot or knowing your abilities even better than you do, will assign you to your place. Whatever the case may be, if you learn all you can about your position and then play it to the best of your ability, you'll never let your team down.

7
tactics

Tactics are all the ways teammates work together to mount an attack or put up a defense. If you've ever played a team game, no one needs to tell you that without well-planned and well-practiced tactics, you really have no hope of scoring a point or keeping from being scored against.

In soccer, as in any other game, the whole subject breaks down into three categories—*individual* tactics, *group* tactics, and *team* tactics.

Individual tactics are those you use by yourself. Group tactics take over when you are joined by one or several teammates. Team tactics, of course, are employed by the entire team. All three types are used whether you're attacking or defending. All three must blend together for a winning effort.

INDIVIDUAL TACTICS

Let's first see the individual tactics that come into play in that always-breathtaking moment when the ball arrives at your feet and you must go on the attack.

Instantly, you're faced with four choices. Perhaps you can kick the ball far downfield to safety. Or pass it immediately to a teammate. Or dribble until you're better positioned for a pass. Or, if you're closely guarded, shield the ball with your body until a teammate races up for a pass.

Your tactics? "Read" your situation—*swiftly.* Then be decisive and make your choice just as swiftly. Keep your head and don't let the surrounding action fluster you into a wrong choice. Once you've made your decision, quickly carry it out; then, if the changing movement of the players around you calls for a new choice, make it without hesitation. And keep the ball under close control as you think. A split second of hesitation or lost control is sometimes all an opponent needs to take the ball away.

Actually, you should not wait until the ball arrives before considering your choices. Be thinking as it approaches. Quickly check your surroundings. With experience, you'll be able to do this in a flash. Perhaps a shout from a nearby teammate will be all you need. Perhaps you'll glimpse your team's colors out of the corner of an eye. All this will enable you to keep keep track of the players around you without ever actually taking your eyes off the ball. Then you'll be ready for whatever you must do—kick, pass, dribble, head, or shield the ball.

Whatever action you choose, carry it out smoothly. Use all the skill you've got. Then, once you've sent the ball on its way, don't stop to congratulate yourself. Don't let down. Watch the action; follow it; be prepared for whatever happens next.

And don't take time to scold yourself if your choice was wrong or your play was poorly made. Rather, make a fast mental note not to make the same mistake again, and then get on with the game. In the next days, you can review your errors and take steps to correct them.

Now let's shift over to your defensive role. Your individual tactics now center on how best to handle the attacker you're assigned to cover.

First, always stay between your opponent and your home goal. You know what happens in football when a defender lets a pass receiver get behind him for a successful catch: In the race that follows, the defender usually loses. The same thing happens in soccer.

Keep your eye on the ball as your opponent plays it. Remember, enemy shoulders and eyes can mislead you with feints. But the ball can't. And try a few feints of your own. Pretend to move in one direction and then, when the dribbler starts in the opposite direction, be *there*, ready and waiting.

When the ball comes to your opponent, don't charge in immediately to tackle it away. The rushed tackle is a common error made by beginners. It is clumsy and is easily avoided. So be patient. Stay with the opponent and wait for just the right moment. The right moment? When the ball is rolling free of the dribbler's feet, and when you're certain you can make the tackle successfully.

At all times, when the ball is being passed to or from your opponent, watch for the chance to intercept it. But take as much care with the interception as with the tackle. In particular, be careful when trying to cut off the ball as it is streaking towards your opponent. Your dash to it may put the opponent behind you and close to your goal. So be certain that you can reach the ball—and certain that there is a teammate close by who can cover the opponent if you miss the interception. Otherwise, guard the opponent and wait for a chance to tackle.

GROUP TACTICS

Group tactics are essential to intercepting, tackling, and passing.

As with the attempted interception, it's best not to try a tackle until a teammate has moved in to back you up. Then, should the dribbler escape your tackle and scoot past to your rear, your teammate will be there to take over the defense. So always try to stall a bit. Block your opponent's path and wait for that shout or glimpse of familiar color that tells you help has arrived.

While waiting, maneuver the opponent toward the touchline so that there is a chance the ball will go out of bounds. If it does— and if the opposition is the last to touch it beforehand—the ball goes over to your side for a throw-in. It's quite as good as a tackle.

Your coach will work you hard at defensive group tactics, showing you how the players in a small group can keep their opponents well guarded and still cover each other. And remember, on plays close to your own goal, one back defender may be assigned to play sweeper, roaming freely behind the other defenders and rushing to be of help wherever there is trouble.

In attacking, three tactics come into play when you pass.

First, of course, never keep the ball too long. It must always go as soon as possible to a teammate better positioned to move it downfield. And that teammate should not waste a second getting into position. The ball travels more slowly when it's dribbled than when being passed from player to player. And so the longer a dribble continues, the greater the danger of a tackle or some other misfortune.

Second, always pass right to your receiver's feet or stockings. You may be tempted to "lead" the receiver by sending the ball out in front of his or her feet so that it can be caught without breaking stride. But this is dangerous. If the lead proves too wide, the receiver may never reach the ball in time. An accurate pass to the feet or stockings is always easily received, very often right on stride. Should the ball go a little off course, it will still be close enough for the receiver to make adjustments and get to it.

Finally, pass the ball with just the right amount of power. A long pass must be driven hard. But a short one needs no more than a good push.

Most beginners have trouble with the short pass; in their excitement, they tend to over-power it. It is then of no use at all. It either whizzes past before the receiver can get to it or arrives so fast that it can't be stopped. So keep a cool head and judge your distance. Power the ball enough to avoid an interception but make sure that it can be easily controlled at the end of its journey.

TEAM TACTICS

The basic team tactic is the team *formation*—the way the players are arranged on the field so that they can best launch their attacks or defend against enemy penetrations. There are many formations used in soccer today, but the ones your team chooses will depend on the type of game your coach wants you to play.

Formations Many coaches put the emphasis on offense; they arrange their formations so that their attack forces are always greater than their defensive ones. Others prefer a more defensive setup; they feel that their chances of winning are better if the opposition is limited to the fewest points possible—preferably none at all. And still others seek a team in which offense and defense are pretty equally balanced.

Though your coach will pick your formations, it will help if you know some of today's most popular ones. They will give you a good beginning idea of what the players must do in any formation.

In Chapter 6, we saw one of modern soccer's most-used formations—the 4–3–3. Illustration 32 shows it again in diagram form, this time with the equally popular 4–2–4. Remember, the numbers start with the back defenders and move upfield to the midfielders and the strikers.

The 4–2–4 puts the emphasis on offense. The four strikers attack along a field-wide front. They are supported by the midfielders. The outside back defenders are also free to attack if it is safe to do so; usually, they go no more than just a short distance up the sidelines. All together, eight teammates can play attacking roles.

The formation, however, is also strong on defense. When the opposition has the ball, the midfielders fall back to defend with the four backs. The two inside backs are almost exclusively defenders. Unlike the outside backs, they are rarely able to attack because they are stationed right in front of their own goalkeeper and net. The area is usually so crowded that they can do nothing more than kick the ball safely away—a vital job in itself!

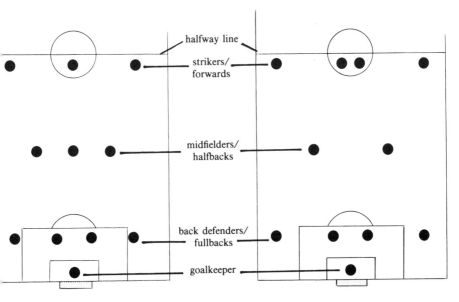

stration 32   *The 4–3–3 Formation*   *The 4–2–4 Formation*

The 4–3–3, with four back defenders, accents the defense. Four backs, aided by three midfielders, defend the goal. Including the goalkeeper, your deep territory is protected by eight players.

As usual, the midfielders have offensive as well as defensive duties. Once the ball is grabbed from the enemy, they take over the attack and move the ball up to the strikers. Then, because there are only three strikers, at least one midfielder must go into enemy territory to give them support. Should the opposition recapture the ball, the midfielder must dash back to his or her own half of the field to play a defensive role again.

The 4–4–2 formation strongly emphasizes defense.

This formation establishes a defense very difficult to penetrate. With four midfielders and four back defenders spread across the field, the opposition is left with little open space for moving the ball.

But it is a formation that works a hardship on the strikers. A lonely two in number, the strikers are sure to be surrounded by opposition defenders. They must play the ball back and forth with extra care if it is not to be stolen away. And they must be experts at delaying tactics that will give their midfielders time to come up and support a drive towards the enemy goal.

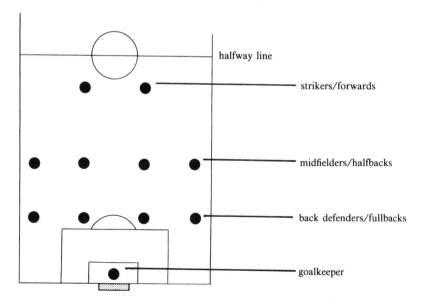

Illustration 33 *The 4–4–2 Formation*

One of the oldest formations is the W–M, so called because, when seen from above, the players form those two letters.

The formation is a pretty balanced one. Five strikers, forming the W, attack along the full width of the field. Three of them are concentrated in the middle and aimed right for the enemy goal. The one in the center is usually the central striker (center forward), the player who is the chief goal maker.

Behind the strikers, five players form the defensive M. The two on the outside are back defenders, and the remaining three are midfielders. Of the midfielders, the two up front are free to move forward and help the strikers. Otherwise, everyone in the M is primarily a defensive player.

The W–M was once used by all soccer teams. Though it has been much replaced by other formations, it is still a favorite of many coaches. Soccer players call it the "granddaddy" of all the more modern formations.

The W–M sharply divides the offense from the defense; for the most part, each group is expected to do only its own work. But today things are changing. The difference between the offensive

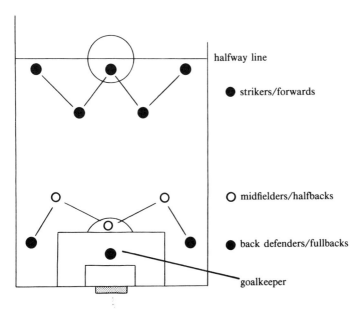

halfway line

● strikers/forwards

○ midfielders/halfbacks

● back defenders/fullbacks

goalkeeper

Illustration 34   *The W–M Formation*

and the defensive player is fast fading away. More and more, the modern player is expected to play both offensively and defensively. The outside back defenders attack in the 4–2–4. The midfielders attack and defend in the 4–2–4, the 4–3–3, and the 4–4–2.

Further, to confuse the opposition, today's players often switch positions as the ball moves up and down the field. A prime example of this kind of play is the *whirl*, which has won great popularity in such countries as Hungary, England, and Brazil. It sets the whole team going in a sort of circular pattern, with the players constantly rotating and switching jobs. It leaves the opposition gasping and almost helplessly confused.

What does all this mean to you? You may never play the whirl, for it is a complex system that the best teams in the world find hard to master, but modern soccer means that you must be prepared to do more than ever before in your team formations. No matter your position, you must learn everything possible about offensive and defensive play. And you must learn something of the duties of the other positions so that, if your coach calls for a switch to confuse the opposition, you'll be able to play skillfully in a new spot for a time.

At the end of Chapter 6, you set an ambitious goal for yourself when you decided to learn and master your position. Now a new goal must be added—to become not only a fine back defender, midfielder, or striker, but the best "all-around" player possible.

On Offense   In football, the advance of the offensive team is easy to follow. Every move begins from a standstill and is made with a "set" play—one that has been painstakingly rehearsed in practice sessions. It may be a pass, a line buck, a sweep, a reverse, or some similar thrust forward.

Soccer, with the ball and the players in constant motion, offers little chance for set plays, though every team has a number on tap for use when the opportunity presents itself. Some, such as the wall pass, are plays of a general nature that can occur at any time in the game. Others, among them the ways for handling the kickoff, are designed to take care of specific game situations.

For the most part, however, the attackers must improvise plays

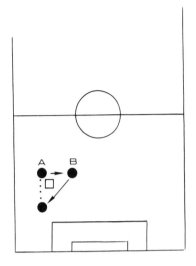

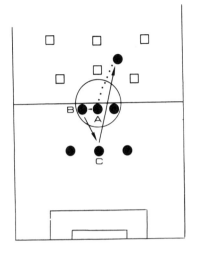

Illustration 35   The *wall pass*. Attacker A has dribbled deep into enemy territory but is threatened by a defender (white square). A passes to teammate B. B kicks again to A, who has run past the defender and is now positioned to approach the goal. The ball travels quickly, giving the impression of being bounced off a wall.

The *kickoff play*. Player A kicks to teammate B, who passes the ball back to C. C fires the ball into enemy territory, where it is received by A. The play enables attackers to keep the ball away from defenders during the kickoff.

as they go along. They must forever be looking for the opportunity to try some on-the-spot play that will move the ball towards a score. That opportunity is most easily found if every attacking players remembers five points:

1. Keep moving at all times and keep looking for new and better spots to send or receive a pass. Constant movement by the attacking unit confuses the defenders. They have no way of knowing where the next attack is coming from.

2. Be ready to take advantage of the changing action. If you're moving in one direction and you see the way blocked there, don't hesitate to go in another—even passing the ball to your rear

if necessary. In fact, deliberately change direction whenever possible. Perhaps the attack is coming down the right touchline and the defenders are shifting in that direction. The time is perfect for a cross kick to a teammate near the left side of the field.

3. Vary your attack between short and long passes so that the defense is never quite prepared for what's coming. Take special care with the long pass, though; the risk of interception is always great. Make sure the ball can reach your distant teammate before a defender overtakes it. Kick powerfully and accurately.

4. Try to assemble the attackers so that they outnumber the defenders nearest the ball. Put two attackers on one defender, or three on two. The ball can then be passed more safely from attacker to attacker. Or the spare attacker can distract the defender while a teammate does the thing most hated by the defense—slips past and heads for the goal.

5. If you're in the midfielder unit, advance the ball by sending it from side to side. Then the defenders can never be certain from which side of the field the ball will suddenly be shot forward to a striker. They will be unable to muster their forces in one area for the interception or the tackle.

On Defense   Two of the same points apply when you're on defense. You need to keep track of the changing action and take advantage of every change. And you need to group your forces so that any attacker with the ball will be outnumbered.

When you join these points with three others, you'll be able to create opportunities for your own on-the-spot plays to regain the ball for your side.

1. Begin your defense as soon as your opponents have the ball. Try your hardest to regain possession before the ball reaches the halfway line and comes into your territory. The closer the ball comes to your goal, the farther it must travel on its way back to a score and the more dangers it will encounter.

2. Pursue the attackers every minute. Never give them a moment's peace. Bother them enough on any attack and they'll soon make a mistake. Bother them enough on every attack and they'll begin to tire—and the mistakes will quickly multiply.

3. If you're a back defender, once you gain possession waste no time in firing the ball upfield. You'll have strikers around you eager to take it away if you give them the slightest chance. Should you be playing an outside spot in the 4–2–4 formation, you might be able to attack upfield a short distance. Do so only if you think it safe; otherwise kick the ball away—fast.

To all these points, two more must be added, one for the attack and one for the defense.

For the attack: Play cleanly, play vigorously, and get that ball into the net.

For the defense: Play just as cleanly, play just as vigorously, and prevent that score.

part three
building your skills

8
let's practice

In one way, soccer is just like all other sports. All its basic skills must be practiced again and again. Only with constant practice can you hope to master them so you can always do them correctly and with ease and confidence.

If you really want to be a good player, these final chapters are especially for you. In Part One, we talked about the many basic skills. Now we're going to talk about the ways top players practice and perfect them.

In this chapter, we'll try exercises you can do by yourself or with friends. In the next, we'll turn to some practice play in *mini-games*. The last chapter will be about how you can put all the exercises and games into a training program that you can follow all year around.

BALL CONTROL

Hardly any of the basic skills will work for you unless your always-busy feet can "handle" the ball just as easily as your hands do in other sports. This is the skill on which all the rest are built. So first things first. Before practicing a kick or a pass, concentrate on teaching your feet to control the ball. See if you can "put some fingers" into them.

To learn ball control, here are five simple exercises. They have helped many new players get the knack of handling the ball no matter what it is doing—and, as you know, it is apt to be doing *anything* in a game. They will give you a good beginning "feel" for controlling the ball while it's rolling on the ground, bouncing here and there, or sailing through the air.

The exercises should be practiced *daily* so that your muscles quickly learn the actions necessary for ball control. At first, you'll probably be able to do each exercise for only a few seconds before the ball skips away. But aim for the day when you can continue any of them for several minutes without interruption. Movements repeated many times non-stop are the best teachers for the muscles.

Exercise: **The Tap**   This is meant to accustom you to having the ball at your feet. Place a ball on the ground and position your feet to either side, setting them twelve to eighteen inches apart. Point your toes straight ahead. Bend your knees slightly and relax.

Now, remaining in place, go up on your toes and hop lightly from foot to foot. Lift each foot about three inches off the ground as you do so. Swing your legs gently from side to side and tap the ball back and forth between your feet. Make sure you always strike the ball only with whichever foot is raised. And try to feel exactly where contact is made. The point of contact should be on the large joint at the base of the big toe.

Each foot must be raised about three inches so that the ball will roll on the ground. If tapped lower, the ball will fly over your opposite foot. If you begin to strike it higher up, you'll likely step right on top of it.

Hold a steady pace and meet the ball softly. Speed and power will come later. Right now, just become accustomed to the gentle, rhythmic actions necessary to send the ball to and fro.

Try to have your feet always come down in the same place after every hop. They will learn a greater control if not allowed to move you forward or backward.

One very important point: Throughout the exercise, keep your head down and watch the ball. You won't be able to do one thing right if your gaze wanders away. Early work on your head position will help you obey soccer's all-important playing rule without even thinking about it: *Always keep your eyes on the ball.*

Exercise: **The Change-of-Pace Tap**   This exercise is simply an extension of the tap. Again, pass the ball back and forth between your feet as you hop, but this time vary your pace so that one day you'll be able to handle balls traveling at any speed. Start slowly and then gradually increase your pace until you are moving as fast as you can. Later, try switching abruptly from speed to speed— perhaps from slow to fast, fast to medium, medium back to fast, and then fast to slow.

You'll need to give special attention to keeping yourself in place and tapping the ball just hard enough to send it to your opposite foot. These aren't the easiest things in the world to do when you're moving at a high speed.

Exercise: **The Tennis-Ball Tap**   Here's a simple but challenging variation of the first two exercises. Substitute a tennis ball for the soccer ball. Because it is so small, the tennis ball will work wonders for your precision and control.

A tennis ball is a favorite item of practice equipment for soccer players. Once they've worked with it for a time, the players claim that the soccer ball is much easier to control because it seems about twice its actual size. Many of the exercises in this chapter can be done with a tennis ball or a handball.

Exercise: **The Juggle**   Agility is needed to control the ground ball. Even more is necessary for getting control of the bouncing or flying ball. Just how much more? The juggle answers that question.

Begin by holding the ball in your hands as you stand with your feet comfortably apart. Next, raise one leg until your thigh is horizontal to the ground. At the same time, bend your knee and let the lower part of the leg hang straight down. Your foot should be horizontal to the ground and pointing straight ahead.

Drop the ball. As it bounces back up, bring your raised foot under it and catch it on the instep. Now, keeping your foot about shin high, bounce the ball lightly up and down. Send the ball only about as high as your bent knee. Remain standing in one spot all the while and, of course, never take your eyes off the ball.

Don't worry if you lose control of the ball and kick it off to one side or the other. You may even send it sailing right over the top of your head. Practice will soon take care of everything.

Exercise: **The Flick**   Your first juggles are easily started by bouncing the ball with your hands. It's a good idea, though, to get into the habit of starting the exercise by flicking the ball into the air with your foot. The movement needed for the flick will add an extra bit of foot control that will come in handy during a game.

For the flick, the ball should be on the ground several inches in front of you. Lightly place the sole of your foot on top of it and then pull the foot and the ball to you. Once the ball is rolling, take your foot away and place it alongside your standing foot. The ball will roll up over the toes of the pulling foot. Immediately turn them up and bring your foot off the ground. The ball will jump straight into the air so that it can be caught and bounced by the instep of your raised foot.

Be sure to practice the juggle and the flick with each foot. All soccer players must be able to handle the ball with either foot, and to do so with equal ease. Always give your "weaker" foot plenty of work. In fact, when doing any exercise, you'll be wise to spend *twice* as much time working with your weaker foot.

KICKING

In Part One, we divided soccer kicks into four basic types—the instep kick, the pass, the volley, and the dribble. The following exercises will help you perfect them all.

Exercise: **The Shadow Kick**   This exercise is done without the ball. All you do is practice the actions of each kick repeatedly until they begin to come easily and naturally. You have no ball to retrieve and so you don't have to stop work between kicks. Remember, your muscles learn an action more quickly if you can repeat it as often as possible without interruption.

Shadow kicking also enables you to practice anywhere and at any time. No yard or field is needed. Your room, a blank wall, the garage, a hallway, the back porch—all quickly become soccer "fields." You can even shadow kick, pass, and volley your way to and from school. True, you'll probably win a few amused glances from passers-by. But who cares? You're perfecting your kicking abilities.

And you need not limit the exercise just to kicking. Practically every soccer skill can be "shadow" practiced.

Exercises: **Kicking for Power and Accuracy**   There is an old saying in soccer that a kicked ball is of no value unless it travels to a spot where it will benefit the team. Accuracy and just the right amount of power are always necessary to send it to that spot. The one aims the ball unerringly towards the spot and the other insures that it arrives right there, neither traveling too far nor fading en route.

From the first days of practice, every player should work for that proper combination of accuracy and power. The exercises in this section will help by calling for you to kick, pass, and volley at targets set at various heights and distances. Some can be done alone and some with a friend.

Instep Kicking: Suppose you want to work on your instep kicks by yourself. If you have a strong back fence or a blank wall, mark it with chalk X's at various heights. Set the ball down about ten feet away, make your approach, and kick to one of the targets. When the ball bounces back, dribble it into place, and make another approach, this time aiming for a new X. Continue the exercise as long as you wish, making sure that every X receives a kick.

Then begin to move the ball closer to and farther away from the wall so that the power of the kicks must be varied to reach the targets.

If you have a vacant lot or a large backyard, mark it with stick targets at various distances. Kick the ball to each target. Then run to the ball and dribble it back to your starting point.

For distance kicks, you'll need a large lot, park, or playing field. Mark your target with a sheet of newspaper held down by a rock or two. Then, from varying distances, kick for the target, seeing how close you can come to it. This exercise really works best with a friend. The two of you kick back and forth to each other, losing no time in collecting the ball.

Passing: When you're by yourself, a blank wall will prove a fine "teammate" for passing practice. Again, draw small X's with chalk, this time all along its base. Then, from varying distances, dribble the ball and pass it to one of the X's. Stop the ball when it bounces back, dribble again, and pass it to another X. For added precision and fun, try substituting that helpful tennis ball from time to time.

Volleying: Again, start with your fence or wall. Standing about ten feet away, throw the ball against your "teammate" and then volley it as it returns. Sometimes volley while the ball is still flying, sometimes while it is bouncing. With practice, you'll be able to get the ball started and then volley it again and again without stopping. In time, try to kick the ball so it flies back at different heights and angles. Before long, you'll be putting your feet everywhere for the volleys, just as you will in a game.

Volley exercises are always fun with a friend. Stand opposite each other at a distance of a yard or two and volley back and forth until there is a miss. It's really a game of catch without using your hands. Incidentally, this exercise can be performed with more than two players. Three players can stand facing each other, two on one side and one on the other. Four players can face each other in sets of two. More than four players can form a small circle and send the ball flying around and across the circle.

All players can add a foot-control exercise to the drill by juggling five times or so on the instep whenever receiving the ball. And, of course, it's a good idea to alternate feet as you go along. Never forget that all-important "weak" foot.

Now some dribbling exercises:

Exercise: **Dribble-and-Weave** When first practicing dribbling, you should move forward in a straight line so you can concentrate fully on perfecting the actions of the dribble. But you'll rarely have the chance to dribble straight ahead for long in a game; an opponent will always be there to get in the way. The dribble-and-weave will prepare you for all the directions you'll have to travel in.

There are many things you can do with the exercise. First, simply dribble up and down the field at varying speeds, weaving to the right and left as you go. Later, follow a weaving path for five yards or so and then try a sharp right- or left-angle cut. Then you could run a curving course that eventually turns into a tight circle; when ready, break out of the circle and go weaving off in one direction or another. These are just a few ideas, and you'll soon think of many others.

And don't forget the tennis ball. It's excellent for sharpening your dribbling and weaving skills.

Exercise: **Partners Dribble-and-Weave**   The dribble-and-weave is particular fun when done by partners. One partner stands in the distance and waves the dribbler forward. Then the partner quickly points out all the directions in which the ball is to be moved. The best partner points quickly and does everything possible to surprise the dribbler.

Illustration 36   **In** *partners dribble-and-weave*, **Caroline points directions for Michael.**

It's even more fun when one partner dribbles while the other serves as an opponent, constantly jumping in the way and trying to take the ball away while the dribbler twists and turns to stay clear.

Exercise: **The Slalom**   Soccer players long ago borrowed this exercise from skiers. (Or perhaps it was the other way around.) Set a number of sticks or garden stakes in the ground, about five to six feet apart, just as if they are the markers on a slalom course in skiing. Then, dribbling at different speeds, weave your way between them, traveling back and forth along the course. Always try to come as close to each marker as you can without touching it.

Exercise: **Dribble-and-Feint**   Just as you'll have to weave while you're dribbling in a game, you'll also have to feint—try all those false moves that fake a looming defender into thinking you're going to escape in one direction when you really plan to move in quite another one.

If you've played football or basketball, you already know the feint. You know how a dip of the shoulders or the head to the left, say, can cause an opponent to move or lean in that direction, giving you the time to scoot away to the right. Even a movement of the eyes can do the same thing.

At first, move ahead along a straight line and pretend that a defender is coming at you from the front. At just the right moment, hesitate, dip your left shoulder, and then dribble to the right. Run a few more steps (here comes another defender!), dip your right shoulder, and move to the left. Now try the head and the eyes. And now see if you can actually lean your body a little in one direction or another.

Work with a partner as soon as you can. A live opponent, cutting in at you from all sides, is much better—and a lot more fun—than an imaginary one.

TRAPPING

There are some very simple ways to perfect your trapping skills when playing by yourself. Again, start with your faithful blank wall. Just roll the ball against it for the foot traps. Then throw it higher for the leg and upper body traps.

Once you've become used to trapping, try exercises that incorporate it with your other skills. Why not combine dribbling, passing, and trapping by running back and forth along the wall while kicking the ball at various chalk marks and then trapping it on its return?

The combined exercises done with a partner provide the most fun, though. Begin by throwing or kicking the ball back and forth to each other and trapping it whenever it comes to you. Each time you kick the ball, use a different type of kick—perhaps a low instep kick first, then a side-of-the-foot pass, and then a lofted instep kick. When throwing, divide your time between the goalkeeper's toss and long and short throw-ins. Then move on to:

Exercise: **Dribble-and-Trap**   The dribble-and-trap will first send the two of you trotting along the field, dribbling, weaving, passing, and trapping as you go. Gradually increase your speed until you're running as hard as you can. Then try all the variations that come to mind.

For instance, dribble, pass, and trap at different speeds. Or run in a straight line for a time and then suddenly weave or charge off in some new direction. Sometimes you or your partner should sprint ahead for a trap; sometimes come close; sometimes dash far away. At some times, concentrate on trapping ground passes; at others, run towards each other and put the ball into the air so the legs or upper body can trap it.

And, for some real fun, substitute that tennis ball from time to time. It will prove as elusive as a chipmunk when you try to trap it.

Throughout the exercise, try to give all parts of the body a chance to trap, and *both* feet the chance to kick.

HEADING AND THROWING IN

If you're practicing headers and throw-ins by yourself, you can put in valuable hours just bouncing a ball off a wall. For the header, you might also try working with the ball suspended by strong string from something overhead, perhaps a rafter or a tree limb. The ball becomes a "punching bag" as it swings back and forth. On low swings, you can practice headers with both feet on the ground. High swings are great for leaping headers.

The best solo heading exercise is the juggle. See how long you can keep the ball in the air by bouncing it with your forehead as you stand still or move about. And, since you're well on your way to developing the basic skills, why not try juggling the ball up and down the length of your body—from the instep to the knee to the head and back again? It's one of the most exciting and valuable exercises in soccer.

Working with a friend, you can head juggle back and forth, seeing how long you can keep the ball going before it drops. Or practice throw-ins from various distances. Also try the throw-in while your partner is on the run. Hitting a moving target is a good accuracy exercise.

TACKLING

Tackling can be shadow practiced when you're by yourself. But, for the best results, tackling practice really needs a partner.

With your partner dribbling very slowly at first, repeat the front, side, shoulder, and sliding tackles until you're thoroughly acquainted with them. The dribbler should not attempt evasive tactics yet, for the whole idea is to give you every chance to concentrate fully on the actions of each tackle.

As soon as you're comfortable making tackles, have the dribbler add the evasive moves. And quicken the pace. Keep right on quickening it until you're doing the exercise at game speed.

Incidentally, so that they could be easily explained, the front and sliding tackles in Chapter 4 were made with the right foot. In a game, though, when you must close in on the dribblers from any direction, you'll be using your left foot just as often to snare the ball. So don't forget to give your left foot equal time in all your exercise sessions. And, of course, practice the shoulder charge from either side.

9
soccer's mini-games

Soccer exercises can be good fun, but the mini-games are even better. And they have other values. They help develop your basic skills more quickly. They give you the feel of what it's actually like to be in a game, for they're real contests in which points are won or lost. They improve your sense of teamwork. And, finally, they provide hours of play that build the strength and stamina needed by every soccer player.

You'll find nine mini-games in this chapter. Try them all. They'll give you the chance to work on each of your basic skills.

Airborne Keep-Away Airborne Keep-Away sharpens your ability to control the ball and to make lofted instep kicks. The game lasts ten minutes or so, and can be played by three to six friends.

Have your friends get into a square area that has sides about ten or fifteen yards long. Place one player in the middle. At the signal "go," the players kick the ball in the air from one to another while the player in the middle tries to intercept it by touching it with any part of the body except the hands and arms (plenty of work on trapping here). For an interception to count, the ball need not be stopped altogether, but has only to be touched.

Whenever there is a touch, the player in the middle trades places with the kicker, and a point is scored *against* the kicker. The player with the fewest points at the end of the game is the winner.

And here's something extra. The ball is allowed to bounce just once after each kick. The receiver must catch it on the instep before or during the bounce. Then the ball must be juggled on the instep until it is kicked away to another player. If the ball bounces more than once or is dropped during the juggle, a point is scored against the receiver.

If you wish, let the player in the middle touch the ball with the hands or the arms on kicks that are too high to be reached by ordinary traps.

Circle Play #1   To learn how to play in crowded quarters during a game, mark out a circle about seven feet in diameter. Then stay within it while you and a partner dribble, pass, and trap. Make the passes difficult and chalk up a point against the partner who steps outside the circle. Ten points puts a player out of the game.

Three or four friends can play the game within a larger circle. Four partners can play against each other in teams of two each. Again, ten points loses the game.

Circle Play #2   This version of circle play sharpens your ability to turn quickly and kick after a trap. Station several players along the perimeter of a circle about fifteen yards across and place one player in the middle. The player in the middle passes to the players on the edge, always turning smartly when the ball returns and passing it off in a new direction. The game can be varied by having the ball kicked several times along the circle's edge before it is suddenly fired into the middle. Whenever the player in the middle misses a trap, that player changes places with the one who made the pass.

You'll need a timekeeper and an assistant off to the side. The timekeeper watches to see how long a player stays in the middle, and the assistant jots down the times. The player who remains in the middle for the longest time without missing a trap is the winner.

Head Racing   This is a fine game for developing your heading ability. On the signal "go," teams of two partners each move out along a course thirty to fifty yards long. One partner walks backward about three or four feet in front of the other, and each team heads the ball back and forth, trying not to drop it. The team that reaches the end of the course in the best time—and with the fewest drops—wins.

If you and a friend are alone, you can run a similar race. Keep track of the drops and of the time it takes to complete the course. Then declare yourselves winners every time you better your record.

Head Soccer   You'll need two teams of three or four players each and a rectangular area about 25 yards long and 15 yards wide. Throw the ball up in the air to start, and then play a regular soccer game, *using only your heads.* Juggle, pass, shoot for goals, and try to take the ball away from your opponents. A point is scored every time the ball goes over your opponents' goal line.

Whenever a player drops the ball, the other team is entitled to pick it up and restart the game. Should the ball go out of bounds, simply "throw" it back in again with a header.

Try playing periods of four or five minutes each, with rests of two or three minutes in between. You'll need the time to catch your breath.

Incidentally, if you have a volleyball court at school, you can play "headers volleyball." The same game can be played on a tennis court.

Corridor Tackling   Three friends can play this game, which takes place in a narrow corridor-like area 20 yards long and about 5 yards wide. Dribbling and passing, two players move back and forth along the full length of the corridor while the third tries to tackle the ball away. Whenever there is a successful capture, the tackler replaces the dribbler who lost the ball. Should the ball go out of bounds, it is immediately kicked back into play and the game continues.

A point is scored for each successful tackle. The player with the most points at the end of ten minutes is the winner. Or the player who first reaches twenty points can be the winner.

Throw-In Keep-Away   Divide your friends into two teams of four or five players each and get everyone into a large rectangular area about 25 yards long and 20 yards wide. Then, using the throw-in only, play a fast game of Keep-Away, whizzing the ball everywhere within the playing area.

This game sounds pretty simple. It is, but not all *that* simple. The players may move anywhere they wish, but any player who receives the ball must obey all the rules of the throw-in, immediately coming to a stop, then throwing the ball with both hands from behind the head and keeping a part of each foot on the ground.

The game quickly sharpens anyone's throwing skills. It becomes quite competitive when you set up goals at either end of the area. Use two sticks, placed a few feet apart, for each goal, and award a point every time the ball is thrown between them.

Moving Goal   This game puts all your soccer skills to work. It should be played in a very large area, even a full soccer field. You need two teams of three to eight players each—plus two partners who are willing to carry a pole between them. The pole can be six to eight feet long.

On the "go" signal, the two teams play a regular soccer game— but a game with a difference!

The two partners hoist the pole to their shoulders and walk all over the field. They become a moving "goal." The teams face the problem of catching up with the goal and then scoring points by driving the ball beneath the crossbar and between the two human goalposts.

A point is scored for each goal. Goal shots may be made from either side of the moving goal. The action lasts for periods of five minutes each. Take two minutes or so off between periods to rest—and to stop laughing.

Crab Soccer   Here is one of the best mini-games in soccer. It can be played with one or several friends and never fails to put each of your soccer skills to use.

Playing with a friend, you both start by sitting on the ground. Then, as if you are doing a spider walk in gym class, lift yourself up on your hands and feet. Keep your back to the ground and raise yourself just a few inches.

Now dribble, kick, pass, trap, and head while scooting all about a square area with ten-foot-long sides. You score points by driving

Illustration 37   Playing *crab soccer*, Caroline passes to Michael.

the ball between goals of two pairs of sticks which are placed on opposite sides of the square.

With several players, try teams of three to six players each. You'll now need an area up to 20 yards long and 10 yards wide. Whenever the ball goes out of bounds, a player throws it back in from a kneeling position at the sideline. You can also play crab soccer with goalies; each kneels in front of a goal and, as in a regular game, is entitled to use hands and arms.

Periods last for five minutes, with a well-deserved rest of two minutes or so between them.

As when you're playing Moving Goal, you'll have to watch out for one thing. With the ball rolling, hopping, and flying here and there, everyone can get to laughing so much that you'll have to stop a bit to catch your breath. So try to be as serious as you can so the game isn't interrupted too often.

10
ready to play

The weeks just before the opening of soccer season are busy. The team practices regularly to become a smoothly functioning unit. The coach drills the players in the skills and tactics that must be used in the coming games. The players work to condition themselves for competitive play.

There are always some players who seem "ahead" of everyone else during the practice sessions. They seem ready for a game right away and never need to lose precious time in bringing themselves up to playing standard. They don't run out of breath during exercises and team drills. They aren't plagued by sore and aching muscles. And they haven't lost the knack of dribbling, kicking, and trapping in all the long months since last season.

In all, they give the appearance of having practiced the entire year.

Well, that's exactly what they *have* done, for it's the only way to be truly ready for the season. On their own, they've worked hard and steadily. They've perfected their playing abilities, built their strength and stamina with the skill exercises and the mini-games, and added to their strength and stamina with other, more general exercises.

Right from the start of the season, they are the most valuable players.

So that you, too, can always be ready for the season, this chapter is about a program of soccer training you can follow all year around. Into it can go all the skill exercises and games you've learned. Let's start by talking about general exercises.

STRENGTH AND STAMINA

Strength, of course, is necessary for tackling, for trapping, and for powerful and accurate kicking. Stamina—"staying power"—enables you to play long and hard without growing too tired. It is a must in soccer, for most players move at a run for over three quarters of every game.

One of the best ways to build strength and stamina during the off-season is to play another sport. Team games such as baseball, basketball, and softball are good choices because their seasons do not interfere too much with the soccer season. Any individual sport—from gymnastics to tennis, swimming, bowling, and hiking —is just fine.

Any off-season training program should include calisthenic exercises. Push-ups, leg raisers, backbends, and such are fine muscle strengtheners. Alternate toe touches, arm swings, and waist bends give the muscles flexibility. Hops and straddle jumps strengthen the legs and add to your agility. All build stamina.

Fun can be added by using a soccer ball during calisthenic workouts. For instance, try the hop by putting your feet together and then jumping back and forth over the ball. First hop from side to side and then from front to back.

For the leg raiser, sit on the ground with your legs out straight and the ball resting on your ankles. Now repeatedly raise and lower your legs—and the ball. Keep your legs from touching the ground each time they come down.

Push-ups can be done by placing your hands on top of the ball and then moving up and down as usual.

These are just three ways of using the ball in your calisthenic workouts. You'll soon see many others. Why not try an arm swing with the ball held in both hands. Whip the ball in great circles in front of you, carrying it straight up over your head and then down below your waist.

Of course, using the ball or not, you'll avoid stiff and sore muscles if you repeat each exercise no more than five times when you first start working out. As soon as your strength and stamina begin to build, steadily increase the repeats until they number thirty, fifty, or even more.

Illustration 38 *Push-ups with the ball* are like regular push-ups except that both hands are directly under you, on top of the ball.

Running is said to be the best exercise of all for soccer players, and so should be a mainstay of your training program. It quickly strengthens the legs and just as quickly builds stamina. Remember, you're going to be moving at a run most of every game.

Running in place is a fine beginning exercise. Simply go through the motions of running without moving forward. Breathe steadily, pump your arms a bit, and lift each foot six or seven inches off the ground. First run to a count of 20 or 25, counting once each time a foot touches the ground. Then, as your stamina builds, steadily increase the count to at least 50.

You may wish to run long distances, but long-distance running isn't really necessary for the soccer player. You'll be just as wise to work on short-distance exercises that stress the various *kinds* of running used in a game.

One exercise is called Run-and-Stop. You run for about five yards, stop for a second or two, and then run again at a different

Illustration 39   **Sheri and Michael** *run in place.* **Here's one exercise that can be done almost anywhere.**

speed or in a different way. You might try this sequence: *walk*, stop, *trot*, stop, *run sideways*, stop, *run medium hard*, stop, *run backward*, stop, *sprint hard*, and stop. All the while, concentrate on breathing steadily and easily. Soon, you'll be able to go through the sequence and repeat it again and again without panting.

At first, run very short distances and use only three or four different ways of running so you won't overtax yourself. But little by little, increase the distances and add to the ways of running. Stamina is best built by making yourself do a "little more" each day or week.

As soon as your stamina begins to build, you should try the Full Circuit Course, running around the outer edge of a playing field or a vacant lot. It is best tried on a soccer field, but any large area will do.

Start at one corner of the field. *Trot* along the sideline for half the length of the field. Now *run backwards* the rest of the way to the goal line. Next, following the goal line, *sprint* across the field. When you reach the far side, *walk quickly* or *trot* up the sideline to midfield. Then *run sideways* until you reach the other goal line. Finally, *sprint* along the goal line back to your starting point.

On your first day, plan to run the circuit just once, perhaps twice. You'll be out of breath by then. Then add to the distance, a little at a time, each day. You may want to run in a straight line. That's fine, but soon begin to follow a weaving path. Only rarely in a game will you have the chance to run in a straight line for any great distance. So, as when you're dribbling, it's smart to get into the habit of weaving as early as possible.

Remember the slalom exercise in Chapter 7? It's just as good practice for running as for dribbling. Set those sticks or garden stakes about five or six feet apart and then, running at different speeds or changing pace as you go along, weave your way back and forth between them. As you did when dribbling, come as close to each stake as you can without touching it.

Much the same exercise can be done with a series of hula hoops (or bicycle tires or even circles made of string) placed on the ground. Run from hoop to hoop, hopping into each. Always be sure to land and spring away on both feet. Then place the hoops close together so you can hop directly from one to the other.

All these exercises will bring quick results. And results will come all the *more* quickly if you carry out your training program against a background of good health habits.

Get plenty of sleep and always eat nutritious, well-balanced meals. Lunches should feature a selection of fruits, and evening meals an ample serving of vegetables. Avoid in-between snacks of fattening cakes, cookies, and candies. If you must snack, choose a nutritious food—perhaps milk, fruit, or vegetables such as raw carrots.

Smoking and drinking have no place in an athlete's life, especially a soccer player's. To run as you must, you need all the stamina that you can muster. Smoking and drinking do nothing but erode it. And, of course, no one needs to talk of the dangers of drug use.

YOUR TRAINING PROGRAM

Year-around training programs should be carried out every day for at least five or six days of every week. All athletes know that daily work is the very best way to build strength, stamina, and the skills of a sport to a maximum.

But you've learned all sorts of exercises—from the skill exercises and mini-games to calisthenics and running. If you tried them all in one day, you'd never finish before dark. How can they be put into a daily program that will still leave time for school and other activities?

Let's say that you plan to practice Mondays through Saturdays. Between Monday and Friday, concentrate on just two skills each day. If you plan carefully, you'll be able to cover all the skills by the end of the Friday session. It's a good idea to use the ball-control exercises as warm-ups for each day's work. And a good idea to repeat a few of the exercises done on the day before so that your muscles won't forget them. Your schedule for the five days may look like Illustration 40.

With school out, Saturday is a fine day for getting your friends together and finishing off the week's work with some mini-games.

The same schedule can be followed with the calisthenic and running exercises. Work a little on them daily between Monday and Friday. It will add up by Friday.

Before playing the mini-games on Saturday, why not try some of the calisthenic and running exercises on your friends. Some running exercises can be turned into games; for instance, the slalom run makes a fine race. Calisthenics with the ball are always good in a group.

With careful scheduling, you'll be able to fit your entire program into just 35 minutes a day between Monday and Friday. Spend 15 minutes on the skill exercises, 10 minutes on calisthen-

MONDAY	TUESDAY	WEDNESDAY	THURSDAY	FRIDAY
1. *Warm-Up* ball-control exercises	1. *Warm-Up* ball-control exercises	1. *Warm-Up* ball-control exercises	1. *Warm-Up* ball-control exercises	1. *Warm-Up* ball-control exercises
2. *Review* last Friday's exercises	2. *Review* low instep kick dribbling	2. *Review* lofted instep kick passing	2. *Review* volleying foot trapping	2. *Review* heading leg- and upper-body trapping
3. *Basic Skills* low instep kick dribbling	3. *Basic Skills* lofted instep kick passing	3. *Basic Skills* volleying foot trapping	3. *Basic Skills* heading leg- and upper-body trapping	3. *Basic Skills* tackling throwing in
4. *Calisthenics*	4. *Calisthenics*	4. *Calisthenics*	4. *Calisthenics*	4. *Calisthenics*
5. *Running*	5. *Running*	5. *Running*	5. *Running*	5. *Running*

Illustration 40   *Five-day Training Schedule*

ics, and 10 minutes on running. If you can't find a full 35 minutes, it's all right to divide a session between the morning and the afternoon. A full 35 minutes is better, though, for it gives you the time to get warmed up and have a truly good workout.

Thirty-five minutes speed by when you're very busy. Can you really fit all your work into them? You can—providing that you schedule a definite amount of time for each kind of exercise and then stick to that schedule. For instance, here's how your skill exercises for Tuesday might be scheduled:

TUESDAY

1. *Warm-Up*
   ball-control exercises
   (2 minutes)

2. *Review*
   low instep kick
   (1 1/2 minutes)
   dribbling
   (1 1/2 minutes)

3. *Basic Skills*
   lofted instep kick
   (5 minutes)
   passing
   (5 minutes)

Total: 15 minutes

Illustration 41 *Tuesday Skill Exercise.* **Make the most of every exercise minute. Don't get lazy, rest often, or quit too soon. You'll be surprised how much you can do in a few minutes when you put your mind to it.**

Of course, you may work longer than 35 minutes. Extra work is always valuable. But it can be a problem; often, it interferes with other activities and must be stopped. And so short daily stints, concentrating fully on what you're doing, are the best.

No matter how you schedule your sessions, be sure you have practiced all the basic skills by the end of the week. And be sure each day's calisthenics includes as wide a variety of exercises as possible. Check to see that there are some for strength, some for agility, some for muscle flexibility, and so on.

As you ready yourself for work, the following points can help make your program a success:

1. Try to start your sessions at the same time every day. The sessions mean hard work and you can very easily put them aside for some other, more appealing activity unless you develop the *practice habit*. The same starting time each day quickly develops that habit. Once you're used to exercising at, say, four o'clock in the afternoon, you're automatically ready for work at that time and won't feel good about doing something else instead.

2. Try to work in the same place every day. This, too, helps to establish the practice habit. And try to have the place as close to home as possible. A long walk or bike ride may prove bothersome enough to make you skip practice one day soon—and the practice habit starts to go out the window.

3. If you have to miss practice for one or several days, get back to work as soon as possible. With every day you delay, the practice habit grows weaker. If rain cancels your practice, work on those exercises that can be done indoors.

4. If you work with a friend who grows tired of the sessions and finally drops them, don't let yourself do the same thing. Carry on alone until your friend returns or a new partner joins you.

5. Try not to limit all your soccer activity to just the exercise sessions and the Saturday mini-games. Remember, you can dribble and shadow practice anytime—at home, at school, or on the way to the store. Then, as the season draws near, lengthen your sessions as much as possible as a final warm-up for the coming play.

Well, there you have it—your own personal training program. Stick with it and you'll be able to start every season with strength, stamina, and skill. And with something else quite as important: Your enthusiasm for soccer and your confidence in your playing ability will be greater because you have worked so hard to master the game and have earned clear results. In all, you'll be in the best physical and mental condition possible to help your team win its games.

So work hard; be joyful when you win a soccer game, be proud when you lose honorably, and above all, have fun.

That's why soccer was invented and that's why it's the world's most popular game.